Happy Birthday
   Joy -

We Wish you a year of
Happiness and great times ahead
Enjoy reading about our boy's of
Summer that are now in the
history books. Love always
                    Bob & Yuki
                    9/7/14

2ND EDITION

The Cardinals of Cooperstown

Featuring Legends from the Cardinals, Browns, & Negro League Stars

by Greg Marecek and Myron Holtzman

REEDY PRESS

St. Louis, Missouri

Reedy Press
PO Box 5131
St. Louis, MO 63139, USA

Library of Congress Control Number: 2014938007

ISBN: 978-1-935806-75-2

Please visit our website at www.reedypress.com.

Design by Nick Hoeing

Printed in Canada
14 15 16 17 18   5 4 3 2 1

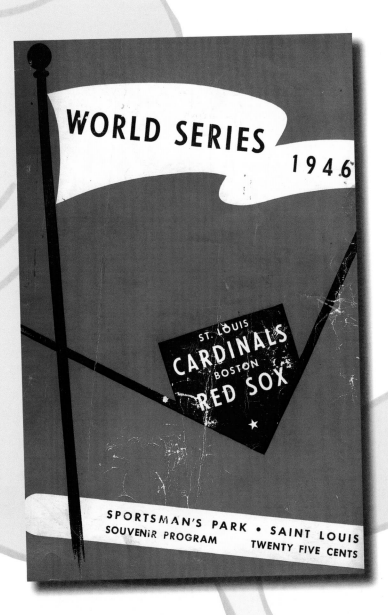

CONTENTS

by Ron Jacober

There are several good "baseball towns" in America. Chicago, Boston, Los Angeles, and New York, to name a few. But the love affair between St. Louis and baseball is unequaled and unique.

Opening Day in St. Louis is regarded as a holy day of obligation. It's almost sinful to ignore it or not care about it. It's Cardinal baseball and there must be something wrong with you if you don't care. Maybe you need to go to confession!

Greg Marecek and Myron Holtzman have revised *The Cardinals of Cooperstown*, with an updated edition. I'm honored they have asked me to write the foreword. Added are three new Cardinal Hall of Famers—Tim McCarver, Joe Torre, and Tony LaRussa. This new edition also includes St. Louis Browns stars Satchel Paige, Goose Goslin, Heine Manush, George Sisler, Rube Waddell, Rick Ferrell, and Eddie Plank and Negro League legends Cool Papa Bell, Willie Wells, and Mule Suttles. All of these wonderful players grace the sacred halls of Cooperstown, not to metion Bill Veeck, who was the   wild-man

promoting owner of the Browns.

I have been a rabid Cardinal fan for as long as I can remember. I grew up sitting on the front porch on warm summer nights listening to Harry Caray describe the exploits of Stan the Man, Red Schoendienst, and Enos Slaughter on the radio. Holy Cow! In fact, in my make-believe games, I was a right-handed Musial hitting game-winning home runs over the garage behind our house. Little did I know then that I would be the only one to interview Caray the day he was fired by Anheuser-Busch.

Little did I know then that I would get to know Stan and call him a friend. I'll never forget the day a bat arrived unexpectedly in the mail autographed: "To Ron – your friend Stan Musial."

Little did I know that one day I would sit next to the legendary Jack Buck in the broadcast booth in Wrigley Field for my first Cardinal broadcast on KSD-TV. In the third inning of that game, Jack, sensing that I was a bit nervous, said: "You want to do some play-by-play, don't you kid?" "Yes," I managed to say. "Well do it," he said, and left the broadcast booth for a couple of innings.

Little did I know that one day I would be doing post-game Cardinal radio shows with Bob Gibson, the greatest Cardinal pitcher in history, or have baseball debates with Whitey and Tony, or have Leo Durocher tell me to "go to hell" as he walked by while I was trying to interview Ernie Banks on a post-game TV show at Wrigley. (Actually what he said was much more obscene than "go to hell!")

I grew up in Highland, Illinois, a small town about thirty miles east of St. Louis. In those days, it was quite a trek to come to St. Louis for a Cardinal or Browns game. We usually made the trip once or, if we were really lucky, twice a year. I remember the first time walking into the park and seeing the field and the expanse of green grass. The ballpark looked so big and that grass so green. So, along with you, I will enjoy this updated edition of *The Cardinals of Cooperstown* and thank Myron and Greg for renewing all those memories for us.

Souvenir World's Series - 1943

SCORE CARD

Cardinals

BUY MORE BONDS FOR VICTORY

THEY WILL TAKE CARE OF YOU TOMORROW

BUY WAR BONDS TODAY

BUY BONDS

by Greg Marecek

Call it updating, call it a sequel, or just call it by the title, this edition of St. Louis baseball Hall of Famers' stories has plenty of new elements for the readers. Since the first edition was published in 2010, we have lost our number one baseball hero, Stan "the Man" Musial, but nationally his light shines even brighter than before. His death reminded a nation of his amazing accomplishments.

The Cardinals have added to their majestic records since 2010. They won their eleventh world championship, defeating the Texas Rangers in 2011, and played in another World Series in 2013, falling to the storied Boston Red Sox. Also, the heir to Stan's throne, Albert Pujols, left for Los Angeles, but be assured he will grace the halls of Cooperstown one day wearing his Cardinals cap.

The main reason for this new volume of the book was to add the three new "Cardinals" entering the Baseball Hall of Fame in 2014, Tim McCarver as the Ford Frick Award winner, and managers Tony LaRussa and Joe Torre, whose 1971 Most Valuable Player season as a St. Louis Cardinal is a further stamp on his Cardinals heritage. Our St. Louis Sports Hall of Fame Committee inducted Torre into its hall in November 2013.

Since changes were being made anyway, my coauthor Myron Holtzman and I realized there was much to expand on as baseball fans of all St. Louis teams in the past. Why not add the Cooperstown members who played for the St. Louis Browns between 1900 and 1953!

After all, right there statistically with the Musial-Hornsby group was a superstar who has the greatest honor a baseball Hall of Famer could be given—he was selected in the very first class of just seven players,

My favorite foursome: from left, Jack Buck, Stan Musial, Greg Marecek, and Whitey Herzog are the first on the tee at Algonquin Golf Club in St. Louis as Marecek hosts a private round with friends.

including Babe Ruth! His name is George Sisler, whose .400 seasons and magic with the glove at first base made him a St. Louis legend.

There are thirteen Browns in the Hall of Fame despite their abysmal record for so many years. As you will see, there are a number of crossover members who played for both the Cardinals and Browns and in every case, their best years were wearing the birds on the bat. Rogers Hornsby, Dizzy Dean, and Sunny Jim Bottomley, to name three.

But not just Cards and Brownies are St. Louis representatives in the hall. There are two more categories: the St. Louis Negro League players from the Stars and Giants and anyone from any team who was born in St. Louis.

By the way, Myron and I are officers of the St. Louis Sports Hall of Fame and ask you to view the lists, stories, and opportunities on the website. Many Cardinals and Browns have been inducted into the city's highest honor in sports.

Finally, thank you to our celebrity testimonials, the Baseball Hall of Fame, the St. Louis Cardinals, the St. Louis Browns Fan Club, and the Negro Leagues Museum in Kansas City, Missouri. Thanks to Nick Hoeing for his incredible design work. Others we may have missed, but we thank you too for your contributions to the creation of this baseball treasure.

This edition is truly the complete history of St. Louis baseball, honoring those who have their plaque in the majestic bastion that is the Baseball Hall of Fame in Cooperstown, New York. Myron and I wish you good reading.

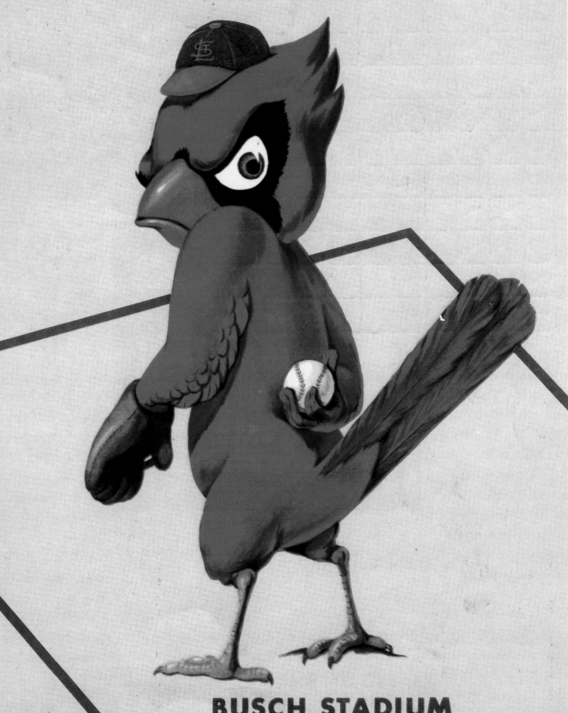

ST. LOUIS *Cardinals* 1956

BUSCH STADIUM

SCORECARD 10¢

The Cardinals of Cooperstown

Featuring Legends from the Cardinals, Browns, & Negro League Stars

CHAPTER 1
COOPERSTOWN
The Home of Baseball

Aerial view of tiny Cooperstown, New York, on the banks of Otsego Lake.

THE MYSTIQUE OF COOPERSTOWN

There is only one road going in and out of Cooperstown, a quaint central New York village nestled along the shore of tranquil Otsego Lake, which is nine miles long and one mile wide. Population 1,898, with one significant main street lined with small shops, almost all of them baseball memorabilia stores or locally owned eateries.

There is a minor league stadium, however. Doubleday Field sits back along the street. It looks right out of the 1920s with bleacher seats from foul line to foul line and close enough to the field for fans to be heard loud and clear!

Why is Cooperstown home to baseball's shrine? Because a man named Stephen Clark asked Major League Baseball's permission to create an attraction to save his fading hometown. He got it in 1936, and the original structure that stands today was built and ready for occupancy in 1939. Oh yes, he was the owner of Singer Sewing Machine Company.

The members of the Baseball Writers' Association of America were selected to vote in worthy inductees, which would surely have included radio and television broadcasters had those areas of technology existed to any large degree at that time.

Much of the heritage has been maintained in the building on Main Street, but of course sizeable modernization has occurred making a tour of the Hall of Fame a lifetime of baseball memories. There is much to see and enjoy.

Besides the plaques, by which you can stand and have your photograph taken, there are three floors and many rooms of amazing, one-of-a-kind artifacts from the turn of the century to today. It gives you chills looking at Babe Ruth's No. 3 jersey, bat, and hat or for Cardinals fans, uniforms, gloves, and the like of Stan the Man, Rogers Hornsby, Lou Brock, Ozzie Smith, and so many more.

The St. Louis Cardinals are no strangers to Cooperstown. At our first writing, there were forty-eight players, managers, broadcasters, and executives elected for induction or awards in the Hall of Fame. Nearly fifteen percent of the total people enshrined have a Cardinals connection and are thus on the St. Louis list!

That number is going up with the addition of three more Cardinals in the class of 2014. A special committee now selects from a list of managers, and this committee gave quick approval to managers Tony LaRussa and Joe Torre, plus broadcaster/player Tim McCarver was given the Frick Award for 2012.

Their Cardinals' resume is rich. LaRussa recently retired with the most wins and longevity as a Cardinals manager. Added to that are three World Series appearances and two world championships with 12 playoff appearances and 4 division titles. Torre's managerial career in St. Louis was brief, but it catapulted him to great success in Atlanta and of course the 4 world

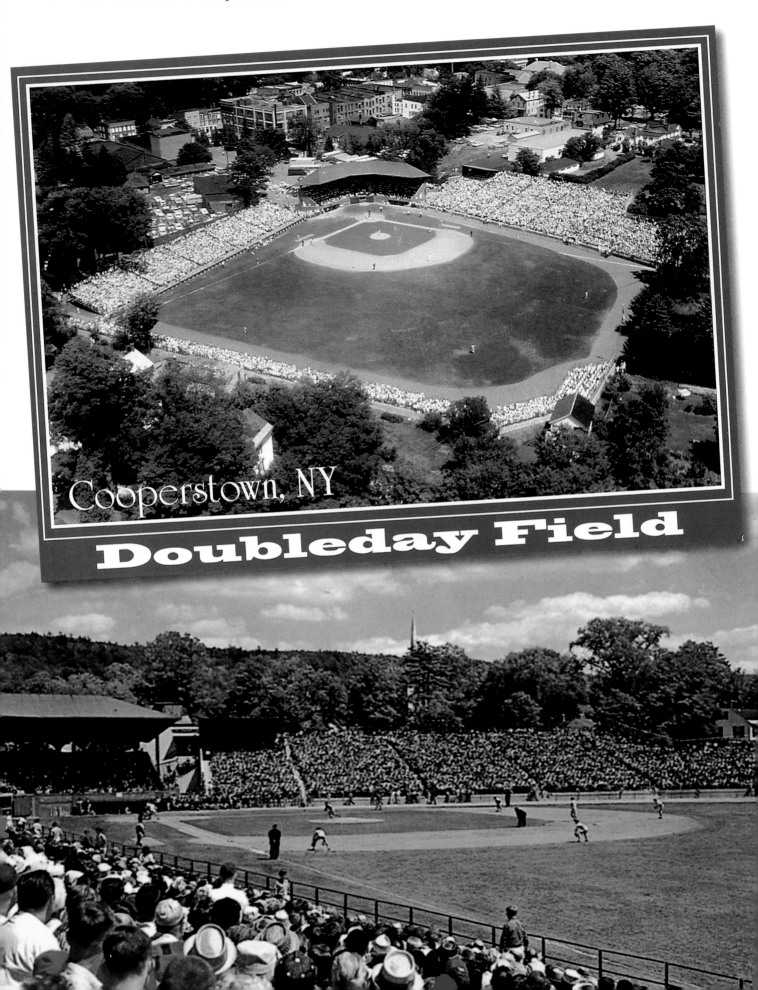

Cooperstown, NY

Doubleday Field

championships in New York. As a player, he made his St. Louis mark, winning the National League Most Valuable Player Award in 1971.

McCarver received the Ford Frick Award for his television broadcasting achievements, but in St. Louis he is remembered as the star catcher of the miraculous 1964 World Series champions. His game-winning homer in Game 6 lives on.

The pilgrimage to Cooperstown is always the last weekend in July when the ranks swell by 15,000 to 40,000, as diehard baseball fans come to see the new honorees. More than fifty living Hall of Famers arrive on Thursday and stay until Monday, walking the streets, greeting the fans, and signing autographs for the local stores.

So put it on the bucket list, whether it be a festive enshrinement weekend or a more quiet time to savor and leisurely soak in the beauty of the region and the grandeur of the museum that brings baseball history alive in Cooperstown.

The historic ballpark in the heart of downtown Cooperstown is home to a minor league team. The field often hosts major league exhibition games, as shown at left.

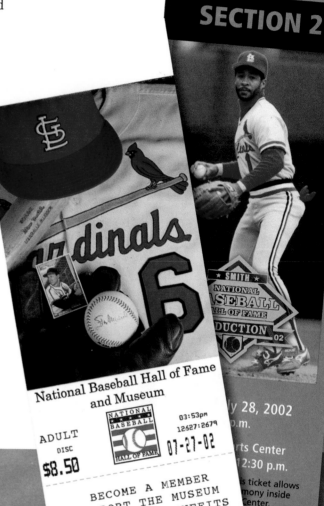

CHAPTER 2
INFIELDERS

BECKLEY, 1st B., Pittsburgs

OLD JUDGE

CIGARETTE FACTORY.

GOODWIN & CO., New York.

BECKLEY, 1st B., Pittsburgs

OLD JUDGE

CIGARETTE FACTORY.

GOODWIN & CO., New York.

1888–1907	G	AB	R	H	2B	3B	HR	RBI	SB	BB	BA
20 Seasons	2389	9538	1602	2934	473	244	87	1578	315	616	.308

Unfortunately for St. Louis, the Cardinals didn't obtain the benefit of Jake Beckley's services until the waning years of his career. Known as Old Eagle Eye because of his ability to hit, Beckley played the last four seasons of his career with the Cardinals (1904–1907). During his twenty years in the big leagues, starting in 1888, he compiled a .308 lifetime average, hit .300 or better in thirteen seasons, and retired as baseball's all-time leader in triples with 244 (he still stands fourth on the all-time list). He held the career record for games played at first base until 1994, when Eddie Murray passed him, but Beckley still leads all first basemen in putouts and total chances.

Born in Hannibal, Missouri, Jacob Peter Beckley was a patient hitter who had the reputation of never swinging at a bad pitch. Later, when he was an umpire, the nickname Eagle Eye took on a new meaning. A hard-hitting first baseman, Jake played minor league baseball for St. Louis in the Western Association before he was purchased by the Pittsburgh Alleghenys (later renamed Pirates) for $4,500 in 1888. He played for the Giants and Reds before joining the Cardinals.

Beckley played seven years in Pittsburgh, averaging .330 per season. He was traded to the New York Giants in 1896 but slumped in 1897 to .250 and was released after only seventeen games. He quickly signed with Cincinnati and pumped up his average to .345. On September 26 he became the last player to hit three home runs in a game until 1922, a few years after the lively ball home-run surge had begun.

Beckley batted .327 for the Reds in 1903, but manager Joe Kelley wanted to play first base, so in February 1904 Cincinnati sold the thirty-six-year-old Beckley to St. Louis. Jake hit well his first two seasons with the Cardinals, batting .325 and .287, but his batting declined quickly as injuries and age began to slow him down.

He served briefly as a National League umpire in 1906 while on injury leave from the Cardinals and tried to play again the following spring. In May 1907 the Cardinals released Beckley, ending his twenty-year career in the majors.

Beckley also loved pulling the hidden-ball trick and tried it on every new player who came into the league. Sometimes he hid the ball in his clothing or under his arm, and other times he hid it under the base and waited for the unsuspecting player to wander off first. One day, with Louisville's Honus Wagner on first, Beckley smuggled an extra ball onto the field and put it under his armpit, partially exposed so Wagner could see it. When the umpire's back was turned, Wagner grabbed the ball and heaved it into the outfield. Wagner lit out for second, but the pitcher still held the game ball and threw Wagner out.

Beckley finished his big league career as the first man to play twenty years without ever being on a pennant-winning team. In addition, the fact that he finished just shy of 3,000 hits kept him out of the Hall of Fame until 1971. None of the voting members had ever met Jake.

JACOB PETER BECKLEY
"OLD EAGLE EYE"
1888 - 1907
FAMED NATIONAL LEAGUE SLUGGER
MADE 2,930 HITS FOR LIFETIME .309 BATTING
AVERAGE . HOLDS RECORD IN MAJORS FOR
FIRST BASE: FOR CHANCES ACCEPTED 25,000
MOST PUTOUTS 23,696, MOST GAMES 2,368.
PLAYED 20 SEASONS WITH PITTSBURGH,
NEW YORK, CINCINNATI AND ST. LOUIS.

JIM BOTTOMLEY

Inducted in 1974 • Years with the Cardinals 1922–1932

1922–1937	G	AB	R	H	2B	3B	HR	RBI	SB	BB	BA
16 Seasons	1991	7471	1177	2313	465	151	219	1422	58	664	.310

When people mention the name Jim Bottomley in Cardinal conversations, they think only of his one spectacular moment, driving in a record 12 runs in one game. It was September 16, 1924, at Brooklyn's Ebbets Field, when the Cards rolled the Dodgers 17–3. Jim had a two-run single in the first, a one-run double in the second, a grand slam in the fourth, a two-run homer in the sixth, a two-run single in the seventh, and a one-run single in the ninth. Ironically, he broke the old mark of the Dodgers' then-manager Wilbert Robinson, who watched as his Baltimore record of 11 RBIs was surpassed.

Robinson could have stopped the assault on his seemingly insurmountable record. Once Bottomley came within a couple of RBIs of the record and with the game well out of hand, the Dodger boss could have simply issued intentional or unintentional walks to Bottomley, but he chose to let his pitchers try to stop the rampage. Asked if he was giving Bottomley a sporting chance to beat the record, Robinson replied, "No, not at all. I just lost count of how many he had!"

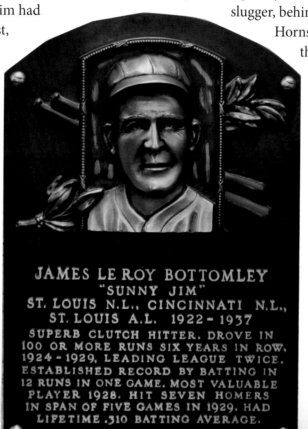

JAMES LE ROY BOTTOMLEY
"SUNNY JIM"
ST. LOUIS N.L., CINCINNATI N.L.,
ST. LOUIS A.L. 1922 - 1937
SUPERB CLUTCH HITTER. DROVE IN
100 OR MORE RUNS SIX YEARS IN ROW,
1924 - 1929, LEADING LEAGUE TWICE.
ESTABLISHED RECORD BY BATTING IN
12 RUNS IN ONE GAME. MOST VALUABLE
PLAYER 1928. HIT SEVEN HOMERS
IN SPAN OF FIVE GAMES IN 1929. HAD
LIFETIME .310 BATTING AVERAGE.

Bottomley—the first real star to come out of general manager Branch Rickey's new Cardinals farm system—was far more than a one-time wonder. Upon his arrival in 1922, the twenty-two-year-old quickly was dubbed the second-best slugger, behind the legendary Rogers Hornsby. He hit .325 in thirty-seven games.

In 1923 the team stumbled, but Bottomley chased Hornsby for the National League batting title in just his first full season, finishing with a .371 mark. He fell back to .316 in 1924 but still produced 111 RBIs, including the 12-RBI day that would stand in baseball's record books until the Cardinals' own Mark Whitten tied it in September 1993 in Cincinnati.

Later declared the Ladies' Day favorite, he went by Sunny Jim, due to his wonderful, fun-loving disposition. As a naive farm boy from Nokomis, Illinois, just coming for a Cardinals tryout, Jim picked up a long, slender bat, looked at it with a puzzled face, and asked, "Who is this Mr. Fungo guy?" Welcome to the big leagues!

Late in his Cardinal career, Sunny Jim

roomed with St. Louis Browns' pitcher Rollie Stiles, who at age one hundred in 2006 was saluted by Major League Baseball as the game's then oldest living player. Stiles, a longtime St. Louisan, recalled his days with Sunny Jim. "He was a terrific roommate and wonderful guy, not to mention one of the greatest ballplayers I was ever around. Our arrangement was perfect, Jim was home when I was on the road with the Browns and vice versa. He definitely had charisma and a fluid style of play at the plate and in the field. We'd get together in the off-season a little, but we had great respect for each other, and he had a super record player!"

Bottomley was a true superstar. In the 1926 world championship season, St. Louis's first in the twentieth century, he was fifth on the team with a .299 batting average, but he was first in the clutch with a league-leading 120 RBIs. The sweet-swinging power hitter won the NL Most Valuable Player Award in 1928, hitting .325 with 93 of his 187 hits for extra bases. In 1928, with the Cardinals winning another pennant with 95 victories, nipping the New York Giants by just two games, Bottomley played a significant role. Besides the average and number of hits, he blasted 31 home runs and drove in 136 runs, both tops in the NL. He had long before been nicknamed Mr. Clutch by admirers and teammates. With the game

on the line, he was the man they wanted at the plate.

A left-handed hitter, Sunny Jim had been helped by Sportsman's Park's generous short porch in right field, but when a screen went up on the pavilion his home run production dropped. However, he could still hit for average, including a .348 mark in limited play during the 1931 campaign. He missed out on the National League batting title by a fraction of a point.

He was traded to the Cincinnati Reds in 1933, stayed for three seasons, and returned for two years to play for the St. Louis Browns. Bottomley died on December 11, 1959, at the tender age of fifty-nine, after sixteen big league seasons. He was inducted in the Baseball Hall of Fame by the Veterans Committee in 1974.

ORLANDO CEPEDA

Inducted in 1999 • Years with the Cardinals 1966–1968

1958–1974	G	AB	R	H	2B	3B	HR	RBI	SB	BB	BA
17 Seasons	2124	7927	1131	2351	417	27	379	1365	142	588	.297

The legacy of greatness was written for Orlando Cepeda well before his career began. After all, Orlando was dubbed The Baby Bull because he was the son of legendary Puerto Rican baseball star Pedro Perucho "The Bull" Cepeda. So all the Latino powerhouse did in his first major league game was homer off Los Angeles Dodger ace Don Drysdale to set the stage for a spectacular career that included nine .300 seasons and a Most Valuable Player Award in 1967 with the World Series champion St. Louis Cardinals.

Orlando Manuel (Penne) Cepeda was only twenty years old when he arrived on the major league scene in 1958 with the San Francisco Giants, en route to Rookie of the Year honors. His manager, Bill Rigney, called him "The best young right-handed power hitter I've ever seen." It was a fitting start to a spectacular career that included eight seasons with 25 or more homers.

Despite being a fan favorite in San Francisco and leading the Giants to the 1962 NL pennant, continued disputes with Giants management forced the team to trade him to the Cardinals for Ray Sadecki in 1966. The slugging first baseman soon was re-nicknamed Cha-Cha in St. Louis because he loved to bring a stereo in the clubhouse to share his beloved salsa music. He quickly became the spirit that sparked the Cardinals to their World Series run in 1967. That season he hit .325, with 25 homers and 111 RBIs, earning the NL MVP honor unanimously.

While Cepeda's life on the field was of Hall of Fame material, his off-the-field life was just the opposite. After retiring as a star from the game he loved, his flame flickered when he was convicted of drug trafficking charges that led to a five-year jail sentence in 1978. Cepeda served only ten months of the sentence, but the drug conviction blotted his baseball career and effectively banned him from baseball for more than twenty years.

Major league officials and sportswriters felt that Cepeda could never regain his former status as a man of character, integrity, and good sportsmanship, and they denied him entrance into the Hall of Fame.

However, Cepeda fought back into the hearts of baseball fans and worked to rebuild his image throughout the 1980s and 1990s. His community work in San Francisco as well as his efforts to promote sports as a way to stay away from bad influences almost completed his journey.

On the final year of his eligibility, Cepeda fell seven votes short for entry into the Hall of Fame. After a three-year waiting period ended in 1996, his name was added to the list of players the Veterans Committee could induct into the hall. In 1999 he was selected for Cooperstown.

Cepeda was recognized nationally for his humanitarian efforts as an ambassador for baseball. He served as an honorary spokesman for the Crohn's and Colitis Foundation of America, and in 2001 won the Ernie Banks Positive Image Lifetime Achievement Award.

CHARLES COMISKEY

Inducted in 1939 • Years with the Brown Stockings 1882–1889, 1891

1882–1889, 1891	G	AB	R	H	2B	3B	HR	RBI	SB	BB	SO	BA
13 Seasons	1390	5796	992	1529	207	68	28	883	416	197	132	.264

His reputation and legacy in baseball always were associated with his achievements as a businessman/entrepreneur who had the foresight to recognize baseball as a major industry in the making in the earliest days. Born in 1859, he would spend his life as a player then owner in the major leagues until 1931.

A right-handed hitting first baseman, he made his mark in St. Louis as the player-manager of the St. Louis Brown Stockings of the American Association starting in 1882. A solid defensive first baseman and steady hitter, the Comiskey career stats show 1,390 games, 5,796 at-bats, 1,529 hits, 207 doubles, 68 triples, 28 home runs, 883 runs batted in, 992 runs scored, 416 stolen bases, and a career .264 batting average.

Actually pretty impressive player stats for a guy saddled with the pressures of being the manager of the team as well. And could he manage! Comiskey engineered what is the most successful four consecutive seasons in St. Louis baseball history—period.

His Brown Stockings dropped the word Stockings and went on to win four straight pennants (1885, 1886, 1887, and 1888), winning the American Association championship in 1886. The "overhand delivery" for pitchers was just implemented, and 1885 was just the second World Series ever played! The Chicago White Stockings of the National League were the Browns' opponent.

There was no champion determined as the series was tied at three games apiece after seven games. Game 2 was disputed as the Browns had stormed off the field in the eighth inning and the game was declared a tie. They split the money.

Comiskey's teams were very good. In '85 their record was 79–33, sixteen games ahead of Cincinnati. In '86 they won by twelve games, as Comiskey's teams

had gained a reputation for nonstop verbal abuse of the opposition and intimidation of the umpires.

It was a wild time, as baseball was still trying to establish its standards and leagues. The '87 Browns had a team batting average of .307 and lost the series, which went fifteen games in ten cities!

Comiskey's last season in St. Louis was 1889, and a series of moves put him into the baseball wars as an owner. He first owned a Minneapolis Western League team in 1895. He moved them to Chicago in 1899 and entered the renamed American League in 1901 as the Chicago White Sox. He owned the club until his death in 1931.

In 1910 Comiskey built the most modern stadium in America and named it Comiskey Park. He was committed to building a championship team as he had in St. Louis. In all, his White Sox won 5 American League pennants (1900, 1901, 1906, and 1917), and the infamous 1919 Black Sox scandal. The team won the World Series in 1906 and 1917.

Despite all his success, Comiskey was known as the cheapest owner in baseball and a cause for the scandal in 1919. His Sox were the easy favorites to win a third World Series with their stars, Shoeless Joe Jackson and Eddie Cicotte. In all, eight players were accused of throwing the series and banned from baseball by Commissioner Kenesaw Mountain Landis.

A little known fact about this baseball legend: Comiskey is credited with being the first player in history to position himself off and behind the first base bag when holding the runner on.

Known as the Baseball Palace of the World, Comiskey Park stood for eighty seasons. He was elected to the Baseball Hall of Fame as an executive in 1939.

ROGER CONNOR

Inducted in 1976 • Years with the Cardinals 1894–1897

1880–1897	G	AB	R	H	2B	3B	HR	RBI	SB	BB	BA
18 Seasons	1997	7794	1620	2467	441	233	138	1322	244	1002	.279

Born in 1857, Roger Connor was the nineteenth-century Babe Ruth. A left-handed batter, Connor was actually more like Hank Aaron in that his home run production was consistent if not prolific. In fact, it took Aaron's breaking of Ruth's record for the statisticians to uncover the slugging career of Dear Old Roger, as he was called by friends.

In his day, Connor was a huge man at 6'3", 220 pounds, with impressive speed and mobility. The majority of his quality playing years were with the Troy Trojans and the New York Gothams/Giants. He spent one year with Philadelphia and then the last four seasons with the St. Louis Browns (later named the Cardinals). His first three seasons with the Cardinals were productive, as he batted .321, .329, and .284 with more than 70 RBIs each year. In 1894 he hit a stunning single-season high of 25 triples.

ROGER CONNOR
TROY N.L., NEW YORK N.L.,
NEW YORK P.L., PHILADELPHIA N.L.,
ST. LOUIS N.L. 1880-1897
POWER-HITTING STAR OF DEAD-BALL ERA.
SET CAREER HOME RUN RECORD FOR 19TH
CENTURY PLAYERS. WON LEAGUE BATTING
CHAMPIONSHIP IN 1885 AND HIT .300 OR
BETTER 12 TIMES. HIT THREE HOMERS
IN A GAME IN 1888 AND MADE SIX HITS IN
SIX AT-BATS IN A GAME IN 1895.

The first baseman, who won world championships with the Giants in 1888 and 1889, was the iron man of his day, playing in 1,083 of a possible 1,100 games from 1880 to 1889. He was one of the league's best at the plate for a twelve-year run from 1880 through 1891, and he led Major League Baseball in career home runs for twenty-six years with 138, until the Babe passed him in 1921. But his 233 triples has been surpassed by only four players in history,

including the great Ty Cobb. He also stole 244 bases. His totals are handicapped by the fact that the league did not even keep stolen base stats in Connor's first seven seasons. His speed was remarkable, considering his size.

Soon after he was traded to St. Louis in 1894, he terrorized the league over ninety-nine games with 791 RBIs while hitting at a .582 slugging clip. In one doubleheader he had eight hits. His Giant teammates felt the wrath of Connor's best game ever, when on June 1, 1895, he went 6 for 6, with two doubles, three singles, and a triple in a 23–2 demolition.

There are two particularly interesting historic footnotes to Connor's career. He reportedly hit baseball's first grand slam, when his Troy team was losing 7–4 with two out and the bases loaded in the ninth inning of a game in 1881. The pitcher was John Lee Richmond, who won 25 games that season, and just the year before he had pitched baseball's first-ever perfect game. Connor also hit a ball over the right field wall and onto 112th Street on September 11, 1886, against Boston. It was the first home run to be hit out of the Polo Grounds. Some New York Stock Exchange members who watched the feat were so enamored that they took up a collection and awarded their New York slugger a five hundred dollar gold watch!

LEO DUROCHER

Inducted in 1994 • Years with the Cardinals 1933–1937

1925, 1928–1941, 1943, 1945	G	AB	R	H	2B	3B	HR	RBI	SB	BB	BA
17 Seasons	1637	5350	575	1320	210	56	24	567	31	377	.247

Leo "the Lip" Durocher made the most out of what he had, including being one of the best self-promoters in sports history. When a career .247 batting average over twenty seasons gets a player into the Hall of Fame, there has to be a lot more to the man. He did contribute to the legendary Bronx Bombers of 1928 as a starter for manager Miller Huggins. Then-Cardinals' general manager Branch Rickey sought out Durocher to complete his infield for the 1934 Gashouse Gang at shortstop. Rickey was chastised for trading future Hall of Fame pitcher Paul Derringer to Cincinnati for the light-hitting, good-fielding Durocher.

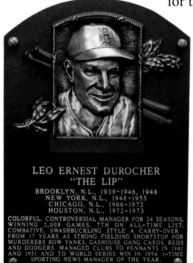

Durocher hit .260 for the 1934 world champion Cardinals, with 62 runs and 70 RBIs. Durocher's irrepressible mouth fit right in with the Gashouse Gang's fiery agitators, who had the arrogance to know that nobody could beat them. Durocher contributed in key spots in the championship season. He had timely hits the final week of the season in a pair of wins that kept the Cardinals tied with the Giants for first place. Then, in the World Series, Durocher's three-hit performance keyed a 4–3 win over the Tigers in Game 6 to even the series at three wins apiece, opening the door to the Cards' dramatic Game 7 triumph. It was the Lip's second ring, not bad for a guy Babe Ruth called "The All-American Out" in 1928, even accusing Durocher of stealing his watch!

In 1939 Leo was named player-manager for Brooklyn, the first of his twenty-four seasons in the dugout. He was perfect for the rambunctious Brooklyn fan base, which was fondly called Flatbush. Leo the Lip was the toast of the town in 1941 when he brought Brooklyn its first pennant in twenty-one years. He followed that success with a 104-win season in 1942, losing the pennant to the Cardinals by two games. In 1946 Durocher's Dodgers met his old Cardinal team again in the National League's first-ever playoff for the pennant. The Cards won two games to none.

At mid-season in 1948, he moved across town to the New York Giants as their new manager, winning the World Series six years later in 1954 over Hall of Fame pitcher Bob Feller and the Cleveland Indians. It too was an upset as Cleveland had won 111 games that season, blowing out the rest of the American League.

The colorful, unpredictable, volatile Durocher managed until 1973, and he was ejected from ninety-five games, second only to John McGraw. Durocher was a dream for the media. His quotes could fill a book, including one for which he is given credit: "Nice guys finish last." How about "Show me a good loser, and I'll show you an idiot" and "Win any way as long as you can get away with it." He was inducted into the Baseball Hall of Fame by the Veterans Committee in 1994, three years after his death.

RICK FERRELL

Inducted in 1984 • Years with the Browns 1929–1933, 1941–1943

1929–1945, 1947	G	AB	R	H	2B	3B	HR	RBI	SB	BB	SO	BA
18 Seasons	1884	6028	687	1692	324	45	28	734	29	931	277	.281

"Brother or no brother . . . he was a real classy receiver. You never saw him lunge for the ball; he never took a strike away from you. He'd get more strikes for a pitcher than anybody I ever saw, because he made catching look easy."
–Wes Ferrell

Wes Ferrell, who won almost 200 games in a fifteen-year major league career, was speaking of his brother, Hall of Fame catcher Rick Ferrell.

For eighteen seasons, parts of seven with the St. Louis Browns, Rick Ferrell was considered one of the best-ever receivers in baseball. In fact, Connie Mack, then manager of the Philadelphia Athletics, elected to play Rick all nine innings of the first-ever All-Star Game in 1933—a testimony to Ferrell, considering that the New York Yankees' Bill Dickey was selected an All-Star that year as well.

When he retired after the 1947 season, Ferrell had caught 1,806 games—more than any other American League catcher, a record that lasted more than forty years.

RICHARD BENJAMIN FERRELL
ST. LOUIS A.L. 1929-1933, 1941-1943
BOSTON A.L. 1933-1937
WASHINGTON A.L. 1937-1941, 1944-1947
CAUGHT MORE GAMES (1,806) THAN ANY OTHER
AMERICAN LEAGUER. DURABLE DEFENSIVE STAND-OUT
WITH FINE ARM. EXPERT AT HANDLING PITCHERS.
MET CHALLENGE OF 4 KNUCKLE-BALLERS IN SENATORS'
STARTING ROTATION. OFTEN FORMED BATTERY WITH
BROTHER, WES. HIT OVER .300 4 TIMES. SECOND
ONLY TO DICKEY IN A.L. CAREER PUTOUTS AT
RETIREMENT.

Richard Benjamin Ferrell was born in 1905, the fourth of seven brothers whose father taught them the game of baseball on a homemade field on the family's 160-acre dairy farm near Greensboro, North Carolina. Rick was the only catcher of the brothers, who all liked to pitch. The brothers played on high school and county league teams, with three later playing pro ball (brother George pitched in the minor leagues).

Rick continued playing baseball at Guilford College, lettering in both baseball and basketball. To pay for his college education, he sometimes turned to boxing. And he wasn't bad with his fists, either, winning 18 of 19 bouts. But baseball was his passion.

The Detroit Tigers signed Rick, but after

being buried in the minors for three years, he gained free agency and signed with the Browns for a huge bonus at the time—$25,000.

It didn't take long for Ferrell to gain the reputation as one of the top receivers in the major leagues, especially his ability to catch knuckleball hurlers.

Browns coach Allan Sothoron reportedly told the *St. Louis Post-Dispatch*: "I don't think there's a better catcher in baseball. I had heard and read a lot about (Ferrell), but he was really better than I believed he could be." In the 1932 season, Rick hit .315, the best among American League starting catchers. He also stroked 30 doubles and recorded 78 assists,

again the most of any AL catcher.

Meanwhile, brother Wes was doing well while pitching for the Cleveland Indians, winning 20 games four years in a row.

"We were brothers off the field, but there was no love lost on it," Rick reportedly said. "We fought like cats and dogs. Wes was always trying to strike me out, and meantime, I was always trying to hit a home run off him."

For instance, when Boston played Cleveland two weeks after the 1933 All-Star Game, Ferrell hit a home run against his brother Wes, who later hit a home run off Boston pitching. It was the first time in major league history that opposing brothers had hit home runs in the same game.

However, in 1933 the Browns, who were looking for cash, traded Ferrell to the Red Sox for players and cash. During those first three-plus seasons in St. Louis, the catcher hit .291 in 408 games.

Rick thrived with Boston and in 1934 convinced Red Sox management to sign his younger brother. For the next three years the siblings formed one of the most dynamic batteries in Major League Baseball history. In 1935 Wes went 25–14, and he won a total of 62 games in three years with Rick as his catcher. From 1933 to 1936, Rick broke Red Sox catcher's records for batting, home runs, doubles, and RBIs. But in June 1937, the brothers were both unexpectedly traded to Washington.

In 1938 he caught big knuckleball pitcher Emil "Dutch" Leonard, giving Leonard a new life in the majors. In 1939 Leonard won 20 games, attributing his regained success to Ferrell's ability to catch the knuckler.

Early in the 1945 season, Rick was traded back to the Browns, where he played several more years before finishing his career in Washington. It was with the Senators in 1944 that Ferrell, now thirty-eight years old, caught four knuckleball

hurlers, the only catcher in major league history to achieve such a grueling feat. Ferrell said he had a strategy when it came to catching the "butterfly pitch": "Never reach for the knuckleball; I just let it come to me."

Ferrell retired after the 1946 season, but came back to catch thirty-seven games for Washington in '47. He became a coach for the Senators and then worked his way up the ranks for Detroit the next four decades as a scout, scouting director, general manager, vice president (1959–1974), and finally, executive consultant (1975–1992) of the Tigers. As an administrator, Rick became the Tigers' "central computer" because he was able to retain vast amounts of baseball information in his "Big Brain," a nickname given him as a player.

The Veterans Committee inducted Ferrell into the Hall of Fame in 1984.

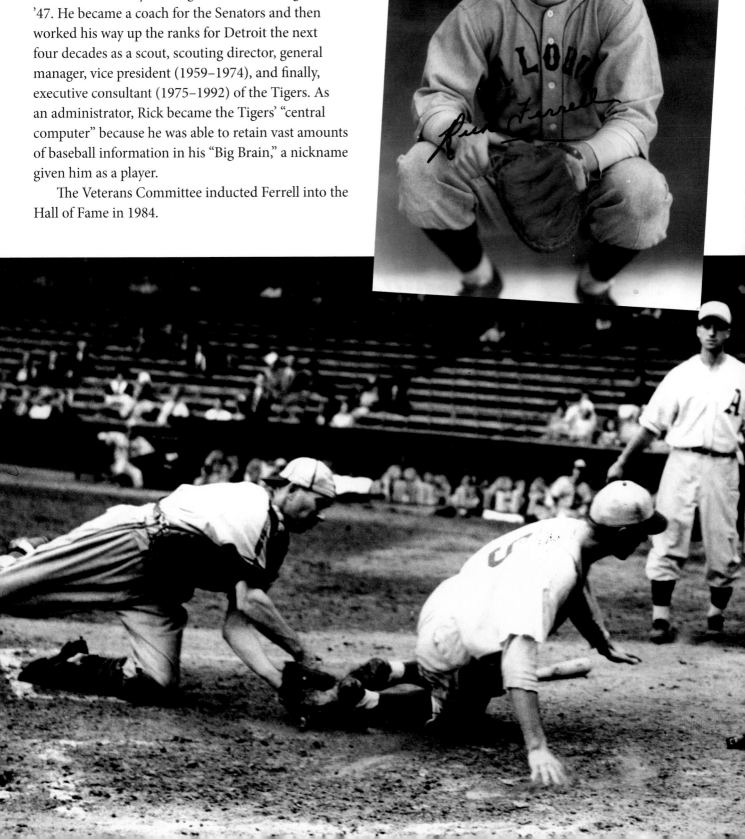

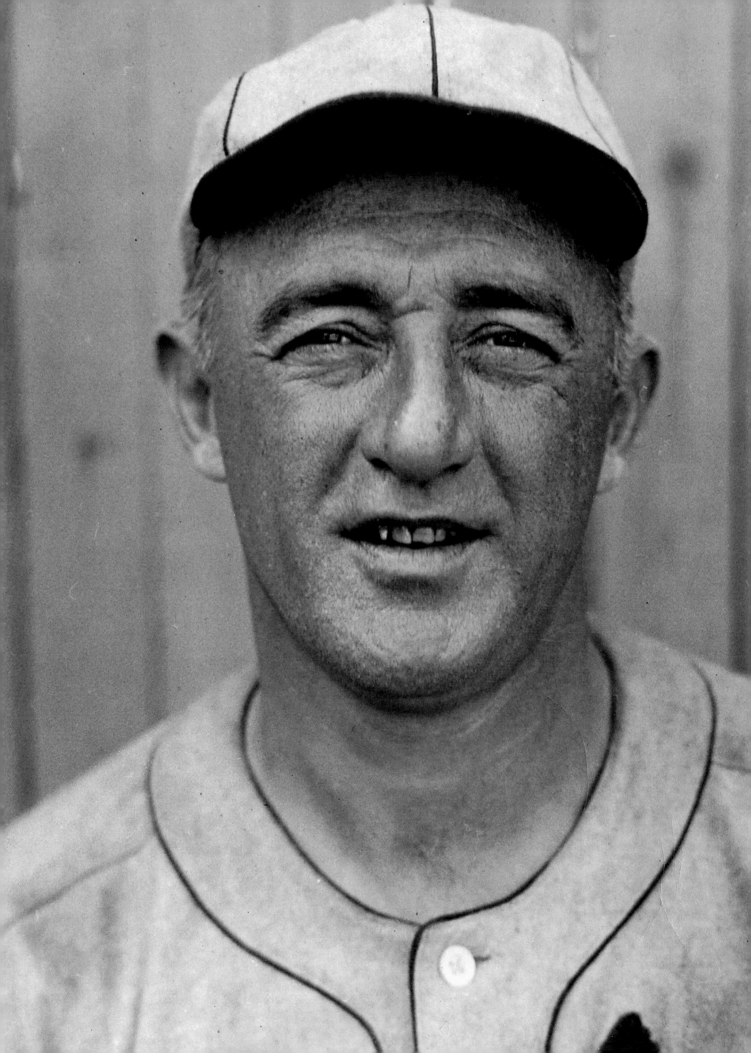

FRANKIE FRISCH

Inducted in 1947 • Years with the Cardinals 1927–1937

1919–1937	G	AB	R	H	2B	3B	HR	RBI	SB	BB	BA
19 Seasons	2311	9112	1532	2880	466	138	105	1244	419	728	.316

The year was 1927. Charles Lindbergh made the world's first solo nonstop flight across the Atlantic Ocean; *The Jazz Singer,* the first prominent talking movie, was introduced; the first long-distance television broadcast became a reality; the Holland Tunnel opened to traffic in New York; and one of the biggest trades in baseball's relatively short history took place.

Fans of the St. Louis Cardinals—and of the New York Giants, for that matter—couldn't believe what they were reading in the papers. Imagine trading the player who had won six consecutive batting titles while averaging .397 over that span. How could it happen? The Cardinals dealt their second baseman and manager, Rogers Hornsby, who had been called the greatest right-handed hitter in baseball, to the New York Giants for Frankie Frisch.

Both Frisch, the infielder who was instrumental in leading the Giants to four World Series appearances, and Hornsby were at odds with their respective managers. After two poor seasons in 1925 and 1926, Giants manager John McGraw let out his frustrations on his captain,

FRANK FRISCH
NEW YORK N.L.1919 - 1926
ST. LOUIS N.L.1927 - 1938
PITTSBURGH N.L.1940 - 1946
JUMPED FROM COLLEGE TO THE MAJORS.
THE "FORDHAM FLASH" WAS AN OUTSTANDING
INFIELDER, BASE-RUNNER AND BATTER.
HAD A LIFETIME BATTING MARK OF .316.
HOLDS MANY RECORDS. PLAYED IN 50
WORLD SERIES GAMES. MANAGED ST.LOUIS
FROM 1933 THROUGH 1938 AND WON WORLD
SERIES IN 1934. MANAGED PITTSBURGH
FROM 1940 THROUGH 1946.

Frisch. McGraw got New York management to deal Frisch (dubbed the Fordham Flash because of his track exploits at Fordham University) to the Cardinals with pitcher Jimmy Ring for Hornsby, who was repeatedly at odds with St. Louis owner Sam Breadon.

When the trade was made, St. Louis fans were furious and ready to string Breadon up by his thumbs.

In fact, the St. Louis Chamber of Commerce denounced the owner by resolution. Fans spread black funeral crepe on Breadon's home and auto agency. Groups threatened to boycott the team.

Replacing the legend didn't bother Frisch. Longtime *St. Louis Post-Dispatch* sportswriter Bob Broeg, who held Frisch in the highest esteem, said, "Frisch didn't make them forget the Rajah, but he made them remember the Flash." In 1927 Frisch nearly brought home the NL MVP honor, with a .337 average and 48 stolen bases. He also set a still-standing major league record for second basemen with 641 assists and a total of 1,059 chances. But even with that spark, the Cardinals narrowly missed winning the NL pennant.

The slashing switch-hitter made up for his lack of home run power with a steady barrage of clutch hits and stolen bases. He was a more consistent hitter when batting left-handed, although he had more power right-handed. Hitting from the left side, he was an adroit bunter and, with his speed when he was young, he often drag-bunted for a base hit. He was especially skilled in punching outside pitches to left field.

> *He was a more consistent hitter when batting left-handed, although he had more power right-handed.*

By the early 1930s, the Cardinals had added a bevy of youngsters, and Frisch faced yet another daunting task: harnessing the talent and temperament of the Gashouse Gang. Frisch, the pilot light of the gang, was named player-manager for the Cardinals midway through the 1933

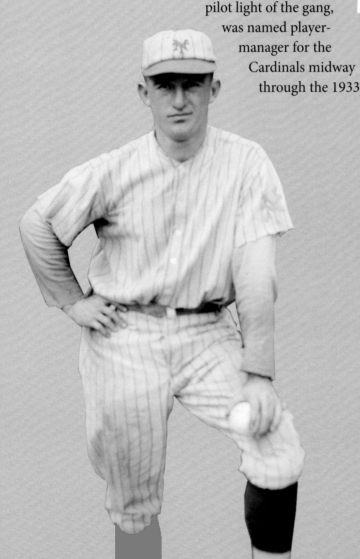

season, when the Cardinals finished fifth. Then, in 1934, the Frisch-led team edged out his former Giants for the pennant and went on to win the World Series over the Detroit Tigers. The colorful 1934 club included such unforgettable characters as pitchers Dizzy and Paul Dean, the inimitable Pepper Martin at third base, Leo Durocher at short, and slugging outfielder Joe Medwick.

The Cardinals won the pennant four times during Frisch's tenure in St. Louis—1928, 1930, 1931, and 1934—with the latter two culminating in World Series titles. Frisch garnered the NL MVP in 1931, and two years later he appeared in the first-ever All-Star Game, hitting the NL's first four-bagger.

Frisch finished his playing career in 1937 with a lifetime average of .316. His career included eight pennants and fifty World Series games. He was elected to the National Baseball Hall of Fame in 1947.

Player-manager Frankie Frisch imparts wisdom to teammate and future Hall of Fame outfielder Joe Medwick.

ROGERS HORNSBY

1915–1937	G	AB	R	H	2B	3B	HR	RBI	SB	BB	BA
23 Seasons	2259	8173	1579	2930	541	169	301	1584	135	1038	.358

"The Rajah," Rogers Hornsby, was arguably the best right-handed hitter in major league history, rivaled by Ty Cobb from the left side. Like it or not, the often gruff, demonstrative, and flamboyant Hornsby was the virtual symbol of the St. Louis Cardinals for twelve seasons. Overall, he spent twenty-five seasons in baseball as a player and manager. His .358 lifetime batting average is the highest all-time for a right-handed hitter in either league. That included a five-year span averaging .400, which has not been approached by any player in history.

Rogers, named after his mother's maiden name, was born in a small town in Texas in 1896 and raised with a farmer's discipline. He began his baseball career as a light-hitting, fair-fielding shortstop in the Texas-Oklahoma League. The owners of his professional contract, the Cardinals, nearly sold him for five hundred dollars after he hit .232 in 1914 but were turned down by a Little Rock ball club. That was luckier than smart.

Over the next two seasons—1915–1916—Cardinal manager Miller Huggins changed Hornsby's stance and swing, and Hornsby himself bulked up twenty-five pounds through an off-season regimen back on dad's farm. It all paid off. In 1916, his first full season in the majors, he recorded a .313 batting average.

In those times, players had no name or number on the back of their uniforms, but beginning in 1917 everyone knew Hornsby and what he could do. He hit .327 and led the National League in slugging percentage and triples, and he was in the top ten in six hitting categories. He did have a hiccup season in 1918, slumping to .281, his last time under .300 until 1932.

He earned his first of six NL batting titles in a row in 1920 with a .370 mark and 218 hits. The fans were coming to see Hornsby, and why not? He destroyed pitchers with seasons of .397, .401, .384, .424, and .403 from 1921 to 1925.

The Rajah's .424 average in 1924 is legendary, but arguably his 1922 season was his best. Cards fans—536,988 of them—came in droves that year to see Hornsby win the Triple Crown with 42 homers (an NL record at that point), 152 RBIs, and a .401 average. He also turned in a .722 slugging average, 141 runs scored, 250 hits, a record 450

ROGERS HORNSBY
NATIONAL LEAGUE BATTING CHAMPION
7 YEARS – 1920 TO 1925; 1928. LIFETIME
BATTING AVERAGE .358 HIGHEST IN
NATIONAL LEAGUE HISTORY. HIT .424 IN
1924, 20TH CENTURY MAJOR LEAGUE RECORD.
MANAGER 1926 WORLD CHAMPION ST. LOUIS
CARDINALS. MOST-VALUABLE-PLAYER
1925 AND 1929.

total bases, and a Cardinal record 33-game hitting streak.

Ironically, great general manager Branch Rickey, who discovered so many hidden talents, was not so successful as the manager of the Cardinals. In 1925, with the Cardinals twelve games under .500,

Rickey was fired by Cards owner Sam Breadon and replaced by Hornsby. Of course, Rogers etched himself into the lineup every afternoon. The manager won his second Triple Crown, with 39 homers, 143 RBIs, and a .403 average. The squad finished in a respectable fourth place with a 64–51 record.

Then it happened—a pennant and first world championship for St. Louis in 1926. This was the year the thirty-three-year-old manager wisely moved himself from second base to right field and acquired journeyman pitcher Grover Cleveland Alexander, who won nine games after arriving at the June trade deadline. The Rajah dropped to a .317 average, battling some back problems and dealing with the issues of managing.

After the euphoria of beating the Bronx Bombers of New York in the World Series, the cheering stopped suddenly when the most popular man in St. Louis was traded to the New York Giants after owner Breadon and Rogers had a strong argument and Hornsby embarrassed the owner by ordering him out of the Cardinals locker room. Then there was the issue of Rogers's insistence on a three-year, $50,000-a-year contract. It was off to New York, the Boston Braves, Chicago Cubs, and back to the Cardinals in 1933.

From 1932 to the end in 1937 his playing time was very limited, including a brief pinch-hitting role

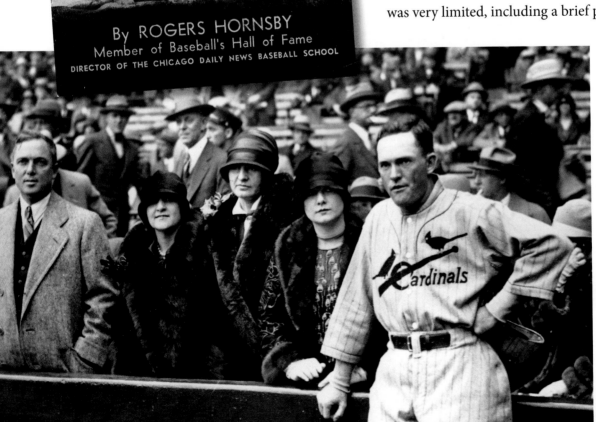

Player-manager Rogers Hornsby poses with Cardinal owner Sam Breadon, far left, and family. The two men—often at odds with each other— wisely kept their distance.

My Biggest Baseball Day

BY

ROGERS HORNSBY

AS TOLD TO THE
CHICAGO DAILY NEWS

THE PEAK OF MY CAREER CAME
IN THE SEVENTH GAME OF THE
1926 WORLD SERIES... AS
PLAYING MANAGER OF THE
CARDINALS, I WON ST. LOUIS'
FIRST PENNANT IN HISTORY AND
BEAT ONE OF THE FINEST OF
ALL YANKEE TEAMS... I PLAYED
A VERY ORDINARY GAME, SO IT
WAS ... HAT I DID, BUT WHAT
... A CHAMPIONSHIP
... WILL NEVER BE

with the Cardinals in 1933. He went on to play and manage the crosstown St. Louis Browns through 1937, retiring after that season, but he returned briefly as manager of the Browns in 1952, and then a year and a half of bad times in Cincinnati.

Not many awards were doled out during his playing days, but Rogers carted off the NL MVP in 1925 and 1929 and made the prestigious *Sporting News* NL All-Star Team in both 1925 and 1926. He died in 1963, and his number (or lack of one) was retired by the Cardinals. Eventually he put the No. 4 on his back, representing his position of second base.

Though the rules of Cooperstown stated a player had to be out of baseball for five years before consideration, Rogers, still an active player, received 105 votes during the shrine's inaugural year. He was inducted in 1942.

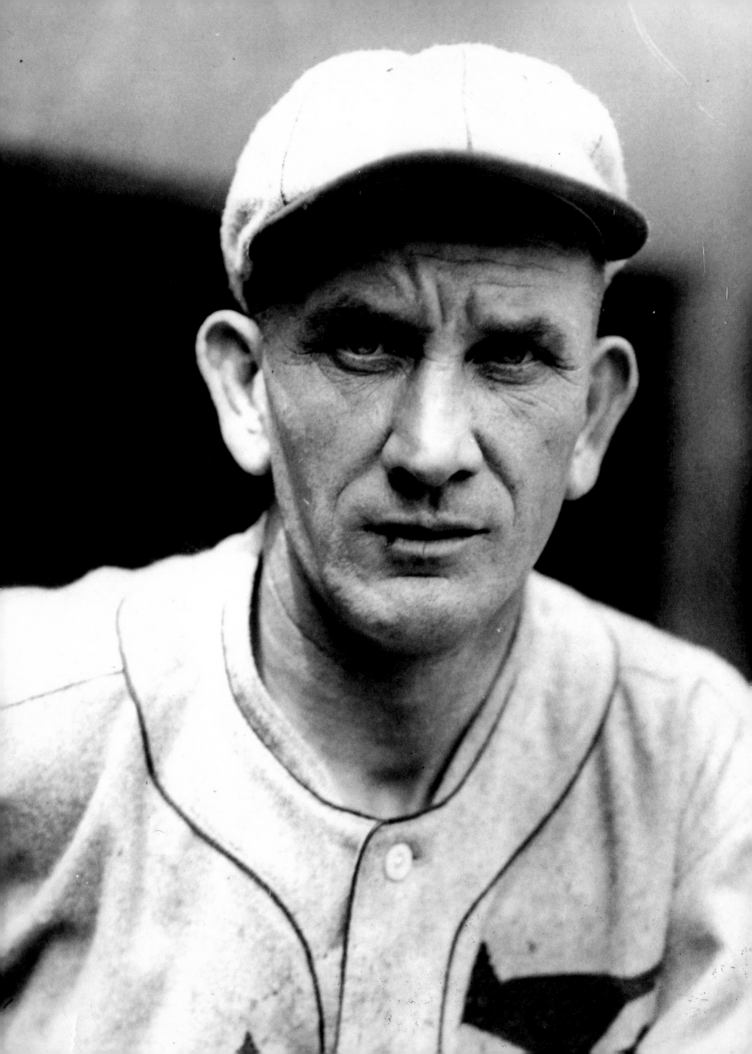

RABBIT MARANVILLE

Inducted in 1954 • Years with the Cardinals 1927–1928

1912–1933, 1935	G	AB	R	H	2B	3B	HR	RBI	SB	BB	BA
23 Seasons	2670	10078	1255	2605	380	177	28	884	291	839	.258

Officially, Walter James Vincent "Rabbit" Maranville was a Cardinal for just two seasons, 1927 and 1928. Although the ball club earned a World Series trip in 1928, to be crushed by the New York Yankees, Maranville did little more than wear the birds on the bat. However, the little man with jets for feet earned his Hall of Fame stripes in his productive years as a Boston Brave, fifteen in all, from 1912 to 1920 and a return stop from 1930 to 1935. He was only 5'5", 155 pounds, when he broke into the big leagues at age twenty in 1912, and it was his speed, quickness, and fielding ability as a shortstop that earned him the nickname Rabbit and a job playing 2,670 games in the National League.

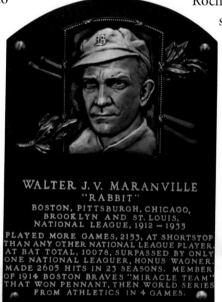

Though his .258 lifetime batting average wouldn't scare anybody, Rabbit was a team leader who could keep a squad loose. A jokester and prankster, he loved to entertain the fans with his antics as much as the ballplayers. On the field, he was more than just durable. He played twenty-three seasons, a National League record until it was broken by Pete Rose in 1986, and led the league several times in putouts and assists.

While he moved to second base once in awhile, his wizardry came at shortstop. Over his lengthy career, he established a record for shortstops, with 5,139 putouts. The Cardinals picked up Maranville in the off-season after he was released by the Brooklyn Robins in August 1926. The Redbirds used him in just nine games late in 1927, after he spent the season at Rochester in the minors. He had also spent part of the 1925 season as a player-manager with the Chicago Cubs. The Cardinals' Branch Rickey saw value in Rabbit as a good veteran to back up star second baseman Frank Frisch. Playing in 112 games for the 1928 NL champions, he hit .240, drove in 34 runs, and in the World Series came through with a .308 batting mark as the Cards were thumped by Babe Ruth and the New York Yankees.

He was purchased by the Boston Braves in 1929 and played five good seasons, hitting .284, .281, and .260 the first three years, where he earned NL MVP votes in four of those seasons. A broken leg ended his career in 1935. He was inducted into Cooperstown in 1954 after thirteen years on the ballot. Unfortunately, that came just months after his death in January of the same year.

JOHNNY MIZE

Inducted in 1981 • Years with the Cardinals 1936–1941

1936–1942, 1946–1953	G	AB	R	H	2B	3B	HR	RBI	SB	BB	BA
15 Seasons	1884	6443	1118	2011	367	83	359	1337	28	856	.312

While Johnny Mize's history shows he might never have been a member of the St. Louis Cardinals, it also shows the Redbirds may well have won more pennants had they not traded him to the New York Giants, where he became one of the National League's great sluggers.

Mize's seventeen-year career, interrupted from 1943 to 1945 for military service, began when the Cardinals signed him in 1930. However, the team attempted to sell Mize to Cincinnati in 1934, two years before he reached the majors, but the trade was overruled by the commissioner, who claimed he was damaged goods, suffering from a painful spur in his groin. Fortunately, the Cardinals doctors rectified the injury.

A big man at 6'2", 210 pounds, Mize hit the ground running during his rookie season in 1936, spelling the injured Rip Collins at first base. In 126 games, he banged out a .326 batting average with 19 homers and 93 runs batted in, which earned him a starting spot for 1937.

Mize had two distinctive habits. He was the first player ever to wear black smudges under his eyes to ward off sun glare, and while at bat he would never step out of the batter's box. He inherited a superb batting eye and won a batting title, three RBI titles, and four home run titles, knocking one out of every NL ballpark.

His nickname, the Big Cat, was given in recognition of his smooth fielding skills around the first base bag. The author of the nickname was a teammate, Buddy Blattner, who later became famous in his own right for tagging stars of the National Basketball Association's St. Louis Hawks—such as Hall of Famers Bob Pettit, Cliff Hagan, and Slater Martin—with a bevy of nicknames.

With the Cardinals for six seasons (1936–1941), Mize had an outstanding batting eye, and he formed a vicious duo at the plate with teammate Joe Medwick. The mighty Mize set a torrid pace but was still blown away in 1937 by Medwick's NL Triple Crown–winning season. Mize hit .364 that season with 25 home runs and 113 RBIs, finishing second in the NL in doubles, hitting, slugging, and total bases, but the Cards still finished in fourth place.

Although the aura of the Gashouse Gang

JOHN ROBERT MIZE
"THE BIG CAT"
ST. LOUIS N L , NEW YORK N.L.,
NEW YORK A. L , 1936-1953
KEEN-EYED SLUGGER SMASHED 359 HOME RUNS
AND BATTED .312 IN 15-YEAR CAREER WHILE
TOPPING .300 MARK NINE SEASONS IN A ROW.
SET MAJOR LOOP RECORDS BY HITTING THREE
HOMERS IN A GAME SIX TIMES AND TRIO IN
SUCCESSION ON FOUR OCCASIONS. WON N.L.
BATTING TITLE ONCE, LED OR SHARED LEAD
IN HOMERS AND SLUGGING PCT. FOUR TIMES,
RUNS BATTED IN AND TOTAL BASES THRICE

was slipping away in 1939, the Big Cat was just getting started. That season began a streak of three straight years when the Georgia native, who hit left-handed but threw right-handed, would have a slugging percentage over .600. As the Cardinals were transitioning with new stars like Enos "Country" Slaughter and the Cooper brothers, Walker and Mort, the Big Cat was carrying the offense. The team had risen from sixth place and 71 wins to second place and 92 wins, just 4½ games behind the pennant-winning Cincinnati Reds.

Mize had two distinctive habits. He was the first player ever to wear black smudges under his eyes to ward off sun glare, and while at bat he would never step out of the batter's box.

Hearing the whispers from demonstrative general manager Branch Rickey that he still wasn't showing enough power numbers, Mize rectified that problem in 1940. He blasted a career-high 43 home runs, a Cardinal record that stood until Mark McGwire came along. Mize led the NL in homers, RBIs with 137, and slugging percentage at .636. His batting

average dipped to .314 amid all those big swings, and now management complained about that! The team finished third, sixteen games off the pace.

Rickey made a mistake in December 1941 when he let his impatience with Mize's injuries get the best of him. He sold Mize for $50,000 to the New York Giants and had to use a platoon at first base to compensate. The Cardinals would have championship seasons in 1942, 1943, and 1944, but some felt that if Mize had remained a Cardinal the team not only would have won those titles but would have added championships in 1945, 1947, and 1948, where a little more offense might have changed those second-place finishes.

As a Giant, Mize continued to pound the league's pitching after his return from World War II. He was back at the top of his game, blasting career-high and league-leading totals of 51 homers, 138 RBIs, and 137 runs scored in 1947. His final five seasons with the crosstown New York Yankees were inglorious for him personally, but he did enjoy playing on five world championship teams. In 1949 the thirty-nine-year-old became a New York hero. He began by winning Game 3 with a two-run, bottom-of-the-ninth single to beat Brooklyn, 4–3. He would lead all players in the series with a .400 average and several big base hits.

Recognizing his incredible offensive production and steady glove over what some saw as limited play over fifteen seasons, the Veterans Committee inducted Johnny Mize into the Baseball Hall of Fame in 1981.

Johnny Mize demonstrates a favorite pose with his Hollywood looks.

1945–1963	G	AB	R	H	2B	3B	HR	RBI	SB	BB	BA
19 Seasons	2216	8479	1223	2449	427	78	84	773	89	606	.289

When speaking of the most remarkable major league careers, one has to mention the ever-popular Red Schoendienst. A player, manager, and longtime coach, the redhead spent seven decades in uniform, mostly as a member of the St. Louis Cardinals. But freckle-faced Schoendienst had to overcome adversity twice to get to the Hall of Fame.

Born in Germantown, Illinois, near St. Louis, Albert Fred "Red" Schoendienst grew up in a large family. His father worked in the mines and on state highway jobs. Red, meanwhile, liked the outdoors, often skipping school to go hunting or fishing or playing his favorite sport, baseball. But it was while working in a Civilian Conservation Corps job at age seventeen that his first setback occurred. He was struck in the left eye by a ricocheting nail, causing blurred vision.

Unfazed, Schoendienst hitchhiked to a St. Louis tryout camp, and the Cardinals signed the nineteen-year-old for seventy-five dollars a month as a shortstop. The following season, while playing at Rochester, he was named the

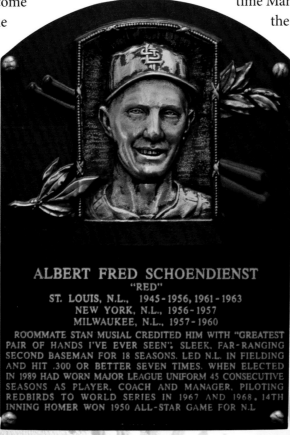

ALBERT FRED SCHOENDIENST
"RED"
ST. LOUIS, N.L., 1945-1956, 1961-1963
NEW YORK, N.L., 1956-1957
MILWAUKEE, N.L., 1957-1960
ROOMMATE STAN MUSIAL CREDITED HIM WITH "GREATEST PAIR OF HANDS I'VE EVER SEEN". SLEEK, FAR-RANGING SECOND BASEMAN FOR 18 SEASONS. LED N.L. IN FIELDING AND HIT .300 OR BETTER SEVEN TIMES. WHEN ELECTED IN 1989 HAD WORN MAJOR LEAGUE UNIFORM 45 CONSECUTIVE SEASONS AS PLAYER, COACH AND MANAGER, PILOTING REDBIRDS TO WORLD SERIES IN 1967 AND 1968. 14TH INNING HOMER WON 1950 ALL-STAR GAME FOR N.L.

International League's most valuable player. He entered the army in 1944 but was discharged prematurely when his eye problem, an injured shoulder, and the first signs of a tuberculosis bug began to slow him down. He joined the Cardinals a few months later as a starting left fielder (at the time Marty Marion was manning the shortstop position), and finished the 1945 season with an NL-leading 26 stolen bases.

It didn't take long, however, for the switch-hitting Schoendienst to move into the Cardinals' starting second-base slot. Lou Klein, the Cards' regular second baseman in 1946, unexpectedly jumped to the Mexican League, and the lanky six-foot Schoendienst slid right in. With sure hands and quick reflexes, he led all NL second basemen in fielding average that season, the first of seven times he earned that honor. In 1950 he handled 320 consecutive chances without an error, and in 1956 he set a league record with a .9934 fielding average at second base. He wasn't too shabby at the plate, either, hitting .281 for the 1946 pennant-winning Cardinals.

Schoendienst was one of the best switch-

43

hitters of his day. The story goes that Schoendienst started switch-hitting as a youngster because of his injured left eye. It seems his vision was blurred because his nose kept him from seeing breaking balls from right-handed pitching very well.

Schoendienst was one of the best switch-hitters of his day.

In 1948 Red doubled his pleasure in record fashion during three consecutive games. On June 5 Schoendienst slugged three doubles and a single against Brooklyn. The following day against Philadelphia in a doubleheader, he slugged three doubles and a homer in the first game and followed that with two more two-base hits in the second game. The

eight doubles in three consecutive games set a major league record, as did his seven extra-base hits in two successive games.

In the 1950 All-Star Game, Schoendienst came in as a late-inning replacement for Brooklyn's Jackie Robinson and reportedly called his shot when he hit a dramatic fourteenth-inning home run to win the game for the NL. The redhead also came closest to a batting title in 1953 when he hit .342, finishing second to Carl Furillo's .344.

Midway through the 1956 season, however, the Cardinals traded Red to the New York Giants in a controversial multi-player deal. A year and a day later, Schoendienst was dealt to Milwaukee where he helped the Braves win the 1957 World Series and 1958 NL pennant.

However, he wasn't winning his battle with tuberculosis. After the 1958 series, even though he played incredibly well, his health was failing. Finally, early in 1959, his health was such that he underwent surgery for the disease that doctors had finally isolated. Several months later he was back in uniform.

However, age was catching up with the redhead and he was released by Milwaukee in 1960. The Cardinals signed him, but over the next three seasons he was used mostly as a utility player, pinch-hitting more than playing. In 1963, at age forty, he decided to leave the playing field and accepted a position as a coach for the Cardinals.

He coached under manager Johnny Keane when the Redbirds won the 1964 World Series, but when Keane left in a huff with management to join the New

York Yankees after the series, Schoendienst replaced him and guided the Cardinals for the next twelve years, then a team record. Under his direction, St. Louis won pennants in 1967 and 1968, and defeated the Red Sox in the 1967 World Series.

Friendly and popular, he had an easygoing managerial style. Fired in 1976, he spent two years coaching for the A's before returning in that capacity to the Cardinals in 1979. He again served as Cardinal interim manager for six weeks in 1980 as Whitey Herzog temporarily left the dugout to become general manager, and briefly in 1990 as a replacement after Herzog resigned. Schoendienst stepped back as coach until the 2000s, when his duties were limited to pre-game practice.

He was enshrined in the Hall of Fame by the Veterans Committee in 1989.

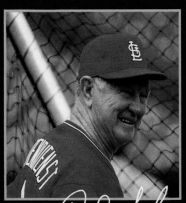

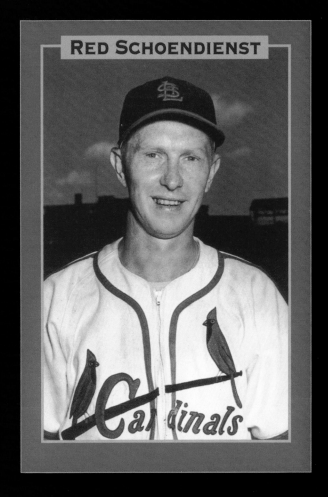

ALBERT FRED "RED" SCHOENDIENST

RED HAS BEEN INVOLVED IN PROFESSIONAL BASEBALL FOR THE PAST 54 SEASONS.

AS A PLAYER, HE APPEARED WITH THE CARDINALS IN 15 SEASONS, MOSTLY AS THEIR SECOND BASEMAN. HE PLAYED IN THREE WORLD SERIES: IN 1946 WITH THE CARDINALS AND IN 1957 AND 1958 WITH MILWAUKEE. HE WAS CHOSEN FOR 10 N.L. ALL-STAR GAME SQUADS, AND IN 1950 CRACKED A GAME-WINNING HOME RUN IN THE 14TH INNING.

HE COACHED IN ST. LOUIS FROM 1961-64. IN 1965 HE BEGAN A 12-YEAR STINT AS CARDINALS MANAGER, THE LONGEST TENURE IN CLUB HISTORY. HE MANAGED THE CARDINALS TO A WORLD SERIES CHAMPIONSHIP IN 1967 AND A NATIONAL LEAGUE PENNANT IN 1968. HE ALSO SERVED AS INTERIM MANAGER OF THE REDBIRDS IN 1980 AND 1990, AND COACHED FOR THE OAKLAND A'S IN 1977 AND '78.

IN 1989, SCHOENDIENST WAS PAID BASEBALL'S ULTIMATE COMPLIMENT WITH INDUCTION INTO THE HALL OF FAME. DURING HIS CAREER, HE COLLECTED 2,449 HITS, INCLUDING A LEAGUE-HIGH 200 IN 1957, BATTED .289, AND TIED OR LED THE LEAGUE IN FIELDING AT HIS POSITION SEVEN TIMES.

TODAY WE HONOR RED BY RETIRING HIS FAMED #2.

RED SCHOENDIENST DAY
SATURDAY, MAY 11, 1996

GEORGE SISLER

Inducted in 1939 • Years with the Browns 1915–1927

1915–1922, 1924–1930	G	AB	R	H	2B	3B	HR	RBI	SB	BB	SO	BA
15 Seasons	2055	8267	1284	2812	425	164	102	1178	375	472	327	.340

If asked to name the greatest player in St. Louis Browns history, it would be hard to argue for anyone other than George Sisler, who has also been called the first great first baseman of the twentieth century.

Needless to say, Sisler was an excellent hitter (he twice led the American League in hitting with .400-plus averages) and fielder. The left-handed hitting first baseman also had speed to burn, leading the AL in stolen bases four times. Oh yes, Sisler also captured the league's Most Valuable Player honors in 1922.

George Harold Sisler, known affectionately as "Gorgeous George," played sixteen years in the major leagues, twelve with the Browns. He finished his career with a .340 lifetime average, hitting more than .300 nine times, including those two seasons in which he hit over .400, making him one of only two players in American League history to hit over .400 twice (the other was Ty Cobb). Many said that he didn't lose anything when the dead-ball era transitioned into the live-ball era.

The son of one of the most prominent

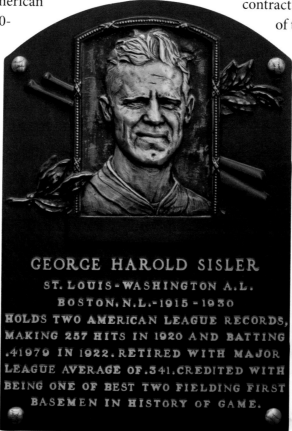

GEORGE HAROLD SISLER
ST. LOUIS-WASHINGTON A.L.
BOSTON, N.L.-1915-1930
HOLDS TWO AMERICAN LEAGUE RECORDS,
MAKING 257 HITS IN 1920 AND BATTING
.41979 IN 1922. RETIRED WITH MAJOR
LEAGUE AVERAGE OF .341. CREDITED WITH
BEING ONE OF BEST TWO FIELDING FIRST
BASEMEN IN HISTORY OF GAME.

families in Nimisilia, Ohio, a small town near Akron, Sisler was a natural athlete. He played several sports, but baseball became his passion.

He was a fireballing pitcher in high school, attracting the interest of several local pro teams and earning several college offers. He signed a contract with the Akron Champs of the Ohio Pennsylvania League, but received no money and never practiced or played a game with the team. That contract was eventually purchased by the Pittsburgh Pirates of the National League.

Acquiescing to his parents' wishes, Sisler enrolled in the engineering program at the University of Michigan with no plans on playing baseball. However, the Wolverines had just hired a new baseball coach, Branch Rickey, who would have a meaningful effect on Sisler's career as well as baseball as a whole.

Rickey, who went on to start the minor league system while general manager of the St. Louis Cardinals, talked Sisler into trying out for the Michigan baseball team and, although only a freshman and unable to play for the varsity, he made a huge impression on Rickey. After another stellar summer in the Akron Industrial League, he made the Michigan varsity his sophomore year. However, after a quick start, he developed arm problems. He continued to pitch, though, and splitting time between pitching and the outfield, earned All-American honors in both his sophomore and junior seasons.

Sisler, meanwhile, continued to be a standout at the plate, hitting .445 and .451 those two seasons and setting his sights on being a professional ballplayer. After weighing offers from Pittsburgh and the St. Louis Browns, Sisler chose the latter because Rickey, his former Michigan coach, was now in the Browns' front office.

Pittsburgh filed a protest because of the contract Sisler had signed while in high school. But Rickey, a Michigan law school grad, had the contract voided because Sisler had signed with the Akron

Champs when he was a minor at age 17 and the contract wasn't cosigned by his father. That loophole gave Rickey his opening to sign Sisler.

As a twenty-two-year-old rookie with the Browns in 1915, Sisler compiled a 2.83 ERA, including a 2–1 victory over future Hall of Famer Walter Johnson. The following day, the reporter for the *Washington Post* reportedly wrote:

"(Rickey) plays him in the outfield and he makes sensational catches . . . he plays him on first base and actually he looks like Chase when Hal was king of the first sackers, and then on the hill he goes out and beats Johnson."

However, Rickey, whom Sisler called "coach" the rest of his career, soon determined that his rookie's future was as a hitter, not a pitcher.

Sisler was converted to an everyday player, taking over as the club's first baseman in 1916. He hit .305 that season, the first of nine consecutive seasons that he hit .300 or better. In 1920 he hit .407 and in 1922 he collected 257 hits, breaking Ty Cobb's record for hits in a single season, while posting a league-leading .420 average. During one stretch, Sisler hit in 41 consecutive games, an AL record until Joe DiMaggio hit in 56 straight games in 1941. Sisler was also second in the AL in doubles (42) and triples (18) and second to Babe Ruth in homers and RBIs in '22.

Those credentials led to the AL's Most Valuable Player honors, the first year an official league award was given.

Sisler never considered himself a home-run hitter.

"Except when I cut loose at the ball, I always try to place my hits," reportedly said Sisler, who had a flat-footed style of hitting. "At the plate you must stand in such a way that you can hit to either right or left field with equal ease."

At the peak of his career, Sisler developed a severe sinus infection that impaired his optic nerve, giving him double vision and chronic headaches, forcing him to sit out the entire 1923 season. He never returned to his level of brilliance after that.

Agreeing to become a player-manager in 1924, he hit .305, then over .300 in five of the following six seasons.

In 1928 the Browns sold Sisler's contract to the Washington Senators, who in turn sold the contract to the Boston Braves, where he became Rogers Hornsby's teammate. With Boston, he hit .340, .326, and .303, before retiring after the 1930 season.

Frankie Frisch, the former Cardinals' Gas House gang member, once reportedly said of George Sisler: "He was poetry in motion, the perfect player."

Sisler's association with sports didn't end upon his retiring from the big leagues. He launched several private ventures, including founding the American Softball Association, and even engineered the first lighted softball park.

In 1942 Rickey hired Sisler as a scout for the Brooklyn Dodgers—another venture that paid off handsomely. One of the players Sisler scouted was Jackie Robinson, who broke baseball's color barrier.

He continued in the Dodgers' front office before moving on with Rickey to Pittsburgh in 1951, instructing young players such as Bill Mazeroski, Roberto Clemente, and Willie Stargell.

Sisler and his wife, Kathleen, had three sons, two of whom played in the majors. Dick spent eight seasons in the big leagues, including several with the St. Louis Cardinals, and later managed the Cincinnati Reds. Another son, Dave, was a big league pitcher

George Sisler was elected to the Baseball Hall of Fame in 1939.

OZZIE SMITH

Inducted in 2002 • Years with the Cardinals 1982–1996

1978–1996	G	AB	R	H	2B	3B	HR	RBI	SB	BB	BA
19 Seasons	2573	9396	1257	2460	402	69	28	793	580	1072	.262

When Jack Buck beseeched the St. Louis radio audience to "Go crazy folks, go crazy," while broadcasting Ozzie Smith's 1985 NLCS home run against Los Angeles, he could have been describing Ozzie's career with the Cardinals. Because Redbird fans were crazy for their Wizard of Oz.

The 150-pound performer provided more entertainment with his glove and acrobatic skills than any Cardinals enthusiast could hope for. For fifteen seasons after Smith was obtained from San Diego in exchange for the Cardinals' recalcitrant shortstop, Garry Templeton, Ozzie's phenomenal play in the field kept Cardinals fans enthralled. His play, often described as part baseball, part ballet, and part gymnastics, enabled him to become a fifteen-time All-Star with thirteen consecutive Gold Gloves.

Still, it was the rather weak-hitting infielder's bat that led to Buck's famous call in that 1985 postseason game. The switch-hitter, who never hit a home run left-handed (he had hit only thirteen in his eight-year career until then), did

the unexpected. With the score tied 2–2 and one out in the bottom of the ninth, he hit a scorcher off the Dodgers' Tom Niedenfuer that ricocheted off the pillar over the right field wall to give the Cardinals the 3–2 victory, which helped launch them into the World Series.

Osborne Earl Smith was born in Mobile, Alabama, and grew up as a star athlete in Los Angeles, California. He honed his baseball talents while attending college at Cal Poly San Luis Obispo. He was selected as a fourth-round draft choice by San Diego in 1977 and made his major league debut a year later. His defensive talents were so outrageously superior that he finished second in the Rookie of the Year balloting to Atlanta's Bob Horner, despite hitting .258 with only one home run.

In 1980 Smith, who many said redefined the shortstop position, set a major league record for assists in a season with 621 and led all shortstops in nearly every defensive category. For his career, Smith ranks first all-time with 8,375 assists and 1,590 double plays. But after the 1981 season, the Padres were willing to trade Ozzie for Templeton—an

OSBORNE EARL SMITH
"Ozzie" "The Wizard"
SAN DIEGO, N.L., 1978-1981
ST. LOUIS, N.L., 1982-1996
REVOLUTIONIZED DEFENSIVE PLAY AT SHORTSTOP WITH HIS ACROBATIC FIELDING AND ARTISTIC TURNING OF DOUBLE PLAYS. THE 13-TIME GOLD GLOVE WINNER SET SIX MAJOR LEAGUE FIELDING RECORDS AMONG SHORTSTOPS, INCLUDING MOST ASSISTS, DOUBLE PLAYS AND CHANCES ACCEPTED. AN EFFECTIVE OFFENSIVE PLAYER, HE ACCUMULATED 2,460 HITS AND STOLE 580 BASES. NAMED TO 15 ALL-STAR TEAMS. HIS RELENTLESS PURSUIT OF PERFECTION HELPED LEAD THE CARDINALS TO THREE WORLD SERIES, INCLUDING A 1982 CHAMPIONSHIP. HIS CONGENIAL PERSONALITY, CONSUMMATE PROFESSIONALISM AND TRADEMARK BACK FLIP MADE "THE WIZARD" A FAN FAVORITE.

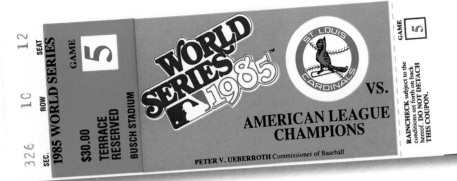

excellent hitter and fielder who had fallen out of favor with Cardinals fans and manager Whitey Herzog. "When Ozzie came over I knew he was a great defensive player," Herzog said. "But he was better than I ever imagined. Every night it seemed like he was taking three or four hits away from the other team with his diving stops. It turned out he was the glue that put our team together. He was the leader on defense and he was also a leader in the clubhouse. You know, players get tired of listening to the manager all the time. So I had Ozzie talk to some of the players and they listened to him."

Herzog also knew of Smith's offensive weakness. After all, Smith only averaged around .230 in his four years with San Diego. In an attempt to improve his hitting and to get Smith to hit ground balls and use his speed, Herzog enticed the Wizard by paying him two dollars for every ground ball he hit. Ozzie, however, had to pay his manager one dollar for every fly ball he hit. "Hell, by July I had paid him more than $300 and I called the bet off," Herzog said. "I never saw anyone work harder than him trying to hit ground balls or line drives."

When he reached base, Smith was dangerous. Twice he stole 57 bases in a season, as the Cardinals go-go offense, led by Ozzie and his buddies Willie McGee and Vince Coleman, became known as Whitey Ball. "I'll tell you what," Herzog said, "in 1987 the biggest winners on our pitching staff won only eleven games. We had all kinds of injuries. But with the defense we had, with Ozzie leading the way, we still managed to win the pennant."

Defensively, Herzog said Ozzie saved an average of 75 runs a season with his incredible talent that saw him make seemingly impossible plays appear almost ordinary. St. Louis fans were so enamored with his defense that they sometimes modified his nickname to the Wizard of Ahs. Ozzie also became the master

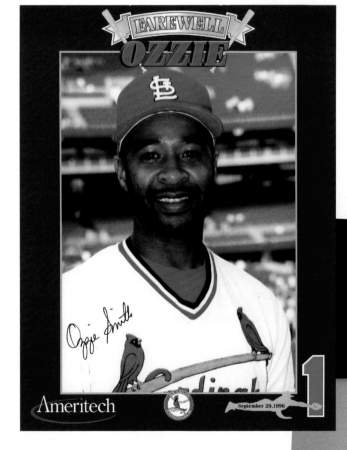

Right: Ozzie addresses the media at his official interview the day before his induction in Cooperstown, 2002.

of the artificial turf at Busch Stadium, often diving for a ball, jumping to his feet, and throwing the hitter out at first. And he mastered the art of throwing on the run and knowing when to bounce the ball to first base, understanding that he would get a true bounce on the artificial surface.

As the seasons progressed, the Wizard improved his hitting. Although still far from a power hitter, Ozzie hit over .280 five times from 1986 to 1993,

including that career-high .303 in 1987 when he also had 87 RBIs for the National League champions. But it was that astonishing defense that put Ozzie into the hallowed halls in Cooperstown. In 2002 the Wizard walked the Yellow Brick Road into a first-ballot selection into the Baseball Hall of Fame.

Inducted in 2006 by Special Committee on the Negro Leagues

Years with the Stars 1926–1931 • Negro Leagues 1923–1944

A true charter member of Negro baseball, George "Mule" Suttles was playing before there was a Negro National League. He was a three-year veteran when the league started in 1921, and he came to St. Louis in 1926.

He went from good to great in his five seasons at Stars Park. Can't go any farther without explaining his popular nickname, "Mule." His big swing, which led to many strikeouts, also led to gargantuan home runs. Hall of Fame teammate Willie Wells tells the story.

"We're playing in Havana, Cuba, at Tropical Park where the center field fence is 60 feet high and over 500 feet from home plate," the tale began.

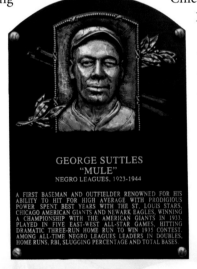

"Suttles hit a low ball, sent it towering to center where it cleared the fence and flew over a group of soldiers on horseback doing crowd control! Never seen anything like it," marveled Wells.

So yes, the nickname was given by his teammates who would shout to Suttles in the batter's box, "Kick Mule!" wanting to see a blast!

His first season with the Stars was 1926, and in the same year the crosstown Cardinals captured their first world championship. Mule Suttles's fabulous season flew under the baseball radar. He clubbed 26 home runs (another source said 15), with a .391 batting average and a .773 slugging percentage. That's no typo!

Suttles was the power in the lineup for the Stars' championships teams in 1928, 1930, and 1931. He hit .371, .344, and .304 in those three seasons, with 20 homers in '28. He performed well in postseason play, overpowering the rival Chicago American Giants in the '28 series.

All-Star games were his forte. Only twenty-seven players were elected to five or more such games and Suttles was one of them, with five. He forever holds the honor of hitting the first home run in All-Star Game history, leading his team to victory.

Instead of Mule, he could have been called Clutch. His five All-Star appearances are legendary. There was a sixth season in which he was selected, but his manager in Newark never got him in the game. His team lost, infuriating teammates and fans.

In all, he posted a stunning .412 batting average, and an equally incredible .883 slugging perecentage. Many considered him the best hitter they ever saw when his team was down a run.

When the Stars folded due to their financial plight, Mule Suttles career began to look like a barnstorming tour. He played for nine teams, and his production didn't wane. He won another championship in Chicago in 1933, with a homer in every 13.5 at-bats.

In the remainder of his long twenty-one-season career, he continued to be a respectable hitter for average with less power production. Suttles ended his baseball life as a manager for the Newark Eagles where he had had three big seasons—.396 and 36 home runs in '36, .420 and 26 homers in '38, and .325 in 1939.

The final validation to Suttles's Hall of Fame credentials was his sterling play in exhibitions against major league squads. In 26 games in 1929 against a team of major league all-stars, Suttles wowed them, hitting five home runs and posting a nearly .400 batting average though records are incomplete.

In one such game, Suttles banged a single, double, and triple against Chicago Cubs star Big Jim Weaver. At the plate for the fourth time, Weaver called time and asked his manager, Leo Durocher, how he should pitch to Suttles.

"You're asking me?" quipped Durocher. "You're the pitcher, I suggest prayer."

George "Mule" Suttles was inducted into the Baseball Hall of Fame at Cooperstown posthumously in 2006.

BOBBY WALLACE

Inducted in 1953 • Years with the Cardinals 1899–1901, 1917–1918

1894–1918	G	AB	R	H	2B	3B	HR	RBI	SB	BB	BA
25 Seasons	2383	8618	1057	2309	391	143	34	1121	201	774	.268

Before Honus Wagner rode onto the scene in Pittsburgh, to be immortalized in the world's most valuable baseball card, baseball's "Mr. Shortstop" resided in St. Louis. His name was Bobby Wallace and he put in twenty of his twenty-five baseball seasons in the Gateway City, split between the National and American Leagues.

Wallace played for a top semipro team from Franklin, Pennsylvania. He was so talented he played nearly every position on the field. In 1894 he signed as a pitcher with the Cleveland Spiders, a team owned by Frank Robison. When Robison purchased Chris von der Ahe's bankrupt NL St. Louis Browns, Wallace was transferred to the newly dubbed St. Louis Perfectos along with fellow future Hall of Famers Jesse Burkett and Cy Young. Wallace found a home in St. Louis.

Wallace, who left the mound after 1896, platooned in the outfield and third base until he settled in at shortstop in St. Louis in 1899. He hit .295 with 108 runs batted in and twelve home runs, second in the league.

In 1902 Robert Hedges bought a floundering baseball franchise in Milwaukee, moved it to St. Louis as the city's second team, and renamed the team the new St. Louis Browns, which went on to be the Baltimore Orioles after the 1953 season. Hedges boldly signed a number of the Cardinals' stars, including Wallace, after the court declared the players "free agents." Wallace moved on to the Browns, which was a loss for the Cardinals

RODERICK J. WALLACE
CLEVELAND-ST. LOUIS-CINCINNATI N. L.
ST. LOUIS A.L. - 1894 TO 1918

ONE OF LONGEST CAREERS IN MAJOR LEAGUES. OVER 60 YEARS AS PITCHER, THIRD-BASEMAN, SHORTSTOP, MANAGER, UMPIRE AND SCOUT. ACTIVE AS PLAYER FOR 25 YEARS. SET A.L. RECORD FOR CHANCES IN ONE GAME AT SHORTSTOP, 17, JUNE 10,1902. RECOGNIZED AS ONE OF GREATEST SHORTSTOPS. PITCHED FOR CLEVELAND IN 1896 TEMPLE CUP SERIES.

and the National League. Wallace had completed another rousing season, hitting .324 and leading the league's shortstops in assists, double plays, and total chances.

Wallace had taken the money but lost being with a contending team, although the Browns did compete for the league title in 1902. His hitting slipped with the Browns, who fell to last place by 1907. His 1908 team contended after taking on a number of fading stars, but they fell short of the pennant. As a Brownie, Wallace had gained the reputation as the game's best shortstop.

It is difficult to measure the talent of the glove with turn-of-the-century players. Wallace was called one of the greatest players of his time. He handled more plays at shortstop than any other player with at least six hundred games in the first decade of the twentieth century, including Hall of Famers Honus Wagner, Joe Tinker, and George Davis.

Wallace had more than 2,300 hits and 200 stolen bases in his long tenure in the league. He hit .268, with 1,057 runs, 34 home runs, and 1,121 RBIs. He coached both the St. Louis Browns (1911–1912) and Cincinnati Reds (1937). He tried managing, but was unsuccessful. He earned the title of "worst manager who managed more than 200 games" with a record of 62 wins and 154 losses. He added umpiring and scouting to his resume, tallying more than sixty years in the pros. Bobby Wallace was inducted into the Baseball Hall of Fame in 1953.

A brilliant shortstop, called one of the three best in the history of the Negro National League, Willie Wells is a name not on the tip of the tongues of present-day baseball fans. However, playing in a city blessed with decades of good professional shortstops, Wells earned his way to the Baseball Hall of Fame as a power hitter, speed merchant, and smooth fielder.

The Stars grabbed Wells from a San Antonio minor league club and away from the Chicago American Giants. His mother wanted him to complete his college degree and thought St. Louis was the place to be.

The St. Louis Giants, the first Negro League franchise in the city, was sold to well-known entrepreneur Dick Kent, who was a real estate mogul and owner of the *St. Louis American* newspaper among many other investments. He would change the team to the "Stars" for the 1922 season.

Wells was a 19-year-old rookie in 1924 who hit a modest .263, not being able to hit the curveball, but in his third season he blossomed. He batted .371 in '26, fourth best in the league, and in 1927 he banged 23 home runs and ranked second in doubles with 20 and fifth in average at .380.

Playing at Stars Park, located at Compton, Market, and Laclede (currently Highway 64/40 near downtown St. Louis), Wells enjoyed the short porch, just 250 feet to a barn that served as the outfield wall. A home run was a ball on the roof!

Wells played on three championship squads in St. Louis—1925, 1928, and 1930—winning more than seventy percent of their games each season.

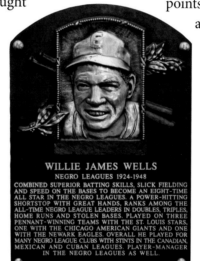

WILLIE JAMES WELLS
NEGRO LEAGUES 1924-1948
COMBINED SUPERIOR BATTING SKILLS, SLICK FIELDING AND SPEED ON THE BASES TO BECOME AN EIGHT-TIME ALL STAR IN THE NEGRO LEAGUES. A POWER-HITTING SHORTSTOP WITH GREAT HANDS, RANKS AMONG THE ALL-TIME NEGRO LEAGUE LEADERS IN DOUBLES, TRIPLES, HOME RUNS AND STOLEN BASES. PLAYED ON THREE PENNANT-WINNING TEAMS WITH THE ST. LOUIS STARS, ONE WITH THE CHICAGO AMERICAN GIANTS AND ONE WITH THE NEWARK EAGLES. OVERALL HE PLAYED FOR MANY NEGRO LEAGUE CLUBS WITH STINTS IN THE CANADIAN, MEXICAN AND CUBAN LEAGUES. PLAYER-MANAGER IN THE NEGRO LEAGUES AS WELL.

He won two batting titles—hitting .368 in 1929 and posting a robust .404 in 1930. In '26, he also set a Negro League record with 27 home runs.

The 1928 series was most memorable for Wells. The Stars had won the first half of the season and the reigning champion Chicago Americans, who had wanted Wells in '22, won the second half. The Stars held on to win the title five games to four, led by Wells's six home runs in the final five games!

In the final championship season of 1930, Wells was superb again. He hit .405 at the plate, five points behind teammate "Mule" Suttles, and led the league in homers with 15 and doubles with 32 and was second in steals with 17.

The Stars folded in 1931, but Wells continued to be a superstar. He played twenty-one seasons and had a lifetime average of .319 (.328 in the Negro Leagues), a slugging percentage of .510, 644 runs scored, 399 runs batted in, 756 games, and 138 home runs, fifth all-time in Negro National League history.

Make no mistake, he was a gifted glove man, rarely making an error. As a player-manager at Newark in 1946, Wells reputedly taught Jackie Robinson how to turn the double play at second base. Wells's fielding prowess had earned him the nickname El Diablo (the Devil) at shortstop. Legend also has it that Willie was the first big leaguer to wear a batting helmet of sorts—a construction helmet—after getting beaned and suffering a concussion.

Willie Wells was inducted in the Baseball Hall of Fame in 1997 by the Veterans Committee. He had passed away at age 84 in 1989.

CHAPTER 3
OUTFIELDERS

JAMES "COOL PAPA" BELL

Inducted in 2006 by Special Committee on the Negro Leagues
Years with the Stars 1922–1931 • Negro Leagues 1922–1946

So who were James Thomas Nichols and "Cool Papa" Bell? One and the same! When James left his birthplace of Starkville, Mississippi, and landed in St. Louis, Missouri, at age seventeen to begin his adult life, he decided to take his father's name, "Bell," as he worked at an independent packing company that later became Swift in 1920. Part of his early life was spent playing baseball with the semipro Compton Cubs of the St. Louis League.

As a crafty left-hander with a nasty curve and knuckleball, he was noticed and signed by the St. Louis Stars of the Negro National League. It wasn't long before the nickname was chosen and became baseball history.

As Bell himself remembered, "We had 12, maybe 15,000 fans in the stands, it was a crucial part of the game and I struck out a slugger named Oscar Charleston. Some of the players thought I looked awful cool out on the mound, not flustered at all, which I wasn't. Then our manager Bill Gatewood heard the crowd saying 'Hey Cool, hey Cool' and he decided it needed another word so he added 'Papa.' That's how the name was born."

In a story similar to that of Stan Musial, a promising young pitcher hurt his arm and was shunted to the outfield. Bell had exceptional speed so despite his weaker arm, he patrolled center field. He made up for it with his ability to catch up with fly balls that looked like they would fall for hits.

Oddly, he was a left-handed thrower but a right-handed batter. He learned to switch-hit after becoming an everyday player, to maximize his speed from the left side. The Negro League game employed more speed and trickery than the major leagues, and Bell could play that style.

Hitting was a challenge in the Negro League, to say the least. Pitchers threw every kind of pitch, legal and illegal, including spitballs, the screwball, and one called the "emery ball," using mud on the seams to make it sink.

Bell once said, "The shine ball was the toughest, the pitchers used Vaseline, and sometimes there would be so much on it, you would blink on a sunny day."

He overcame those obstacles to post a

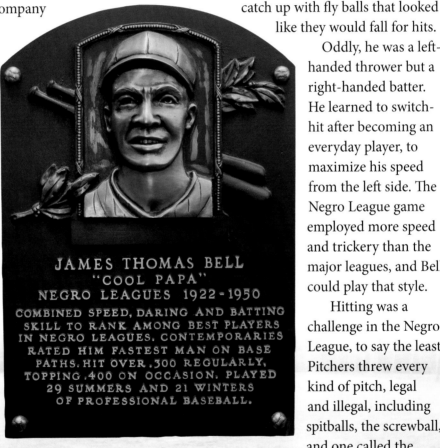

JAMES THOMAS BELL
"COOL PAPA"
NEGRO LEAGUES 1922-1950
COMBINED SPEED, DARING AND BATTING SKILL TO RANK AMONG BEST PLAYERS IN NEGRO LEAGUES. CONTEMPORARIES RATED HIM FASTEST MAN ON BASE PATHS. HIT OVER .300 REGULARLY, TOPPING .400 ON OCCASION. PLAYED 29 SUMMERS AND 21 WINTERS OF PROFESSIONAL BASEBALL.

lifetime batting average of .343 over twenty years in the Negro League, retiring at age 43. His best season was 1926 when he hit .362 after a .354 mark in 1925. Cool Papa played for the Stars, Chicago Giants, Detroit Wolves, Kansas City Monarchs, Pittsburgh Crawfords, and Washington Homestead Grays.

As a crafty left-hander with a nasty curve and knuckleball, he was noticed and signed by the St. Louis Stars of the Negro National League.

The folklore surrounding the colorful Cool Papa begins and ends with stories of his electrifying speed. The most famous saying was created by the great Satchel Paige.

"Cool Papa was so fast, he could turn out the light and be under the covers before it got dark in the room!"

Another Cool Papa legend is that he once hit a ball up the middle and was struck by the ball as he slid into second base! Oddly, he only had 173 stolen bases listed over those twenty seasons.

His seasons in St. Louis were easily his best. Bell led the team to championships in 1928, 1930, and 1931. In a three-year stretch for the Stars, Bell batted .332 in '28, .312 in '29, and .332 in 1930. He had 1,331 hits over his career including 201 doubles. He never played more than 93 games in a season, and in most years he played much fewer.

When the league disbanded after the '36 season due to financial problems, Cool Papa and other big stars fled to the Dominican Republic. Dictator Rafael Trujillo thought a championship baseball team would help his ruling power, and he kept the players under armed guard.

Bell and the others started to feel uneasy about the police presence. What if they didn't win? Would they be shot and killed? Well, never fear, they did win the championship, but barely. A disappointed Trujillo sent them home and disbanded the league for twelve years.

Back in the states, Bell wound up his playing days with the Washington Homestead Grays, and in 1943 he either hit .396 or .356, as the Negro League stats are sometimes different depending on the source.

"Cool Papa was so fast, he could turn out the light and be under the covers before it got dark in the room!"

He finished as a player-manager for some farm teams and then a scout for the St. Louis Browns from 1951 to 1954. He died in 1991 in St. Louis, where a street is named after him. He's on the St. Louis Walk of Fame, and a bronze statue of him stands in front of Busch Stadium with the other Hall of Famers. He was inducted into Cooperstown in 1974, the fifth Negro League player to have been honored.

LOU BROCK

Inducted in 1985 • Years with the Cardinals 1964–1979

1961–1979	G	AB	R	H	2B	3B	HR	RBI	SB	BB	BA
19 Seasons	2616	10,332	1610	3023	486	141	149	900	938	307	.293

There are degrees of Hall of Fame ballplayers, ranging from the on-field greats who lacked off-field character to the smaller number who combined character and dignity with their on-field talent. Louis Clark Brock no doubt takes his place among the classiest of the Hall of Famers.

On the day of Lou's induction in 1985, the distance between Monroe, Louisiana, and Cooperstown must have seemed like tens of thousands of miles. But Lou surely remembered a moment in grade school down South when the discipline of a teacher opened his eyes to the game of baseball. As punishment for throwing a spitball at an unsuspecting female classmate in the fourth grade, young Brock was sent to the library to research and learn something about four baseball players. Those four stars were Joe DiMaggio, Stan Musial, Don Newcombe, and Jackie Robinson.

Lou grew into an excellent high school athlete. In baseball he was primarily a pitcher, but since he possessed only a fastball, hitters made sure the mound wasn't his destiny! Asked about his pitching repertoire one day, Brock smiled,

LOUIS CLARK BROCK
CHICAGO N.L., 1961-1964
ST. LOUIS N.L., 1964-1979
BASEBALL'S ALL-TIME LEADER IN STOLEN BASES WITH 938. SET MAJOR LEAGUE RECORD BY STEALING OVER 50 BASES 12 TIMES AND N.L. RECORD WITH 118 STEALS IN 1974. LED N.L. IN STOLEN BASES 8 TIMES. COLLECTED 3,023 HITS DURING 19 YEAR CAREER AND HOLDS WORLD SERIES RECORD WITH .391 BATTING AVERAGE IN 21 POST-SEASON GAMES.

"Repertoire? Only the express, man, only the express."

Although he earned a football college scholarship to Southern University, the Chicago Cubs lured him away from finishing his degree for a much-needed $30,000 cash bonus after he starred in a pan-American baseball series in 1959.

The Cubs had high hopes for Brock in 1959 after he had one brilliant minor league season, during which he hit .361 with 181 hits, 117 runs, and 33 doubles as the Northern League Rookie of the Year. However, those hopes faded after two big league seasons in which he hit .263 and .258. Brock struggled defensively as well. He did not adapt to right field, particularly in the bright sun of Wrigley Field with all day home games.

Meanwhile, the St. Louis Cardinals were looking for a jolt out of their 1964 doldrums, during which they were sitting in eighth place midway through the season. Gutsy general manager Bing Devine made the move to bring Brock, plus pitchers Jack Spring and Paul Toth, to the Redbirds for former twenty-one-game winner Ernie Broglio, a right-hander who posted a solid 18–8 record with a 2.99 ERA in 1963.

Brock remembers broadcaster Brent Musburger telling Lou the day of the trade, "We're glad to see you go because we're getting a great pitcher in Ernie Broglio!"

"I rub it in every time I see Brent today," Lou said. "He was a rookie newspaper reporter then, and he's a good-natured, great broadcaster today who gets a chuckle out of it too!"

Cardinal manager Johnny Keane inserted Brock into left field and kept the media and fan pressure off his young talent. Brock listened to his elders and stopped trying to be a home run

hitter; instead, he became a line drive hitter and a base stealing wizard. He became the clear catalyst of the 1964 world champion Cardinals, hitting .348 with 146 hits, 21 doubles, 12 homers, and 33 stolen bases with a .391 on-base percentage.

His World Series performance was an omen of things to come. He hit .300 with a home run and five RBIs in the seven-game triumph over the mighty New York Yankees of Mickey Mantle and Roger Maris. In the 1967 and 1968 World Series, No. 20 rewrote the baseball record books. He hit a sizzling .414 and .464, respectively, in a pair of seven-game series, a victory over the Boston Red Sox and a loss to the Detroit Tigers.

Brock was the offensive star of both series. He banged out 12 hits in 1967, another 13 in 1968, and continued his assault on the pitchers and catchers with seven stolen bases in each series. His .391 batting average, with 34 hits in 87 at-bats, is still a World Series record, and his 14 stolen bases tie him with Eddie Collins of the Philadelphia Athletics and Chicago White Sox, who played in the 1920s.

In sixteen seasons as a Cardinal, Lou became the face of the franchise. Known as the Base Burglar, he smashed the stolen base record of Maury Wills by swiping 118 bases in 1974. Brock surpassed the career mark of 892 by Ty Cobb, with a total of 938. Ricky Henderson would later break Lou's major league record.

Brock took pride in being a complete player, and he put a stamp on that fact when he passed the coveted 3,000-hit level in 1979. Perhaps his most satisfying season personally was his last. Playing in 120 games, he hit .304 with 123 hits to finish with 3,023 lifetime.

Four 200-hit seasons, eight .300-plus seasons, a year with 21 home runs, and six All-Star Games are all remarkable numbers, but Lou will tell you his greatest thrill was winning it all in 1964, coming from nowhere the last two weeks of the season. As the chants of "Lou, Lou, Lou" rose to a crescendo, Lou Brock could smile and know he belonged.

JESSE C. BURKETT
Manager Worcester Club

JESSE "THE CRAB" BURKETT

Inducted in 1946 • Years with the Cardinals 1899–1901

1890–1905	G	AB	R	H	2B	3B	HR	RBI	SB	BB	BA
16 Seasons	2066	8421	1720	2850	320	182	75	952	389	1029	.338

Jesse Burkett began his career in the nineteenth century, playing in the big leagues from 1890 to 1905 for the New York Giants (1890), Cleveland Spiders (1891–1898), St. Louis Perfectos/Cardinals (1899–1901), St. Louis Browns (1902–1904), and Boston Americans (1905).

He gained the nickname Crab because of his surly disposition that wore on fans, umpires, and players alike. At a diminutive 5'8", 155 pounds, he was hardly formidable physically.

Though his stay in St. Louis was brief, it was productive. In 1899 the lefty ignited the Perfectos (renamed the Cardinals the following year) offensively, helping to end a streak of seven straight losing seasons. The team finished at 84–67, twenty-eight wins better than in 1898. Burkett came to St. Louis in 1899 along with fellow Hall of Famer Cy Young and a bevy of talented players from the Cleveland Spiders. Cleveland owner Frank Robison purchased the Cardinals and moved his best players to St. Louis while relegating the worst to Cleveland. In 1899 the Spiders went 20–134, the worst record in major league history.

In 1899 Burkett hit a whopping .402, but he still finished second in the batting race to Philadelphia's Ed Delahanty at .408. In 1901 Burkett became the first Cardinal in history to win a league batting championship with his .376 mark. Prior to St. Louis, he had a remarkable run in Cleveland—twice batting over .400. In 1895 he batted .405 and in 1896 Jesse hit .410 with 240

JESSE C. BURKETT
BATTING STAR WHO PLAYED OUTFIELD FOR THE NEW YORK, CLEVELAND AND ST. LOUIS N.L.TEAMS AND THE ST.LOUIS AND BOSTON A.L.TEAMS. SHARES WITH ROGERS HORNSBY AND TY COBB THE RECORD OF HITTING .400 OR BETTER THE MOST TIMES.ACCOMPLISHED THIS ON THREE OCCASIONS.TOPPED THE N.L.IN HITTING THREE TIMES, BATTING OVER .400 TO GAIN THE CHAMPIONSHIP IN 1895 AND 1896.

hits in 133 games played. Only Burkett, Rogers Hornsby, and Ty Cobb had three seasons hitting over .400 in baseball history. There is a dispute over Burkett's .402 year in St. Louis, and some sources put his average at .396. The Baseball Hall of Fame, however, recognizes the .402 average. Burkett had 2,850 career base hits.

The Cardinals were shocked in 1902 when Burkett and five others bolted from the team and landed with the new in-town rivals, the revived and well-financed St. Louis Browns, who had come from Milwaukee in the American League. Burkett began to slide with the Browns, batting over .300 only once in three seasons. He finished quietly in Boston.

Burkett registered pitching highlights early in his career. As a minor league pitcher, he won 27 games in 1888 for Scranton, Pennsylvania, and an eye-popping 39 games with 6 losses for the Worcester Club of the New England League. At Cleveland, he played in two championship series, both against Baltimore. In 1895 his Spiders won the Temple Cup, an 1890s postseason series, behind three wins from Cy Young. Burkett had won Game 1, scoring the winning run in the bottom of the ninth.

The Crab holds an unusual major league record: 55 inside-the-park home runs. He was inducted into the Baseball Hall of Fame as a player by the Old Timers Committee in 1946 and died at age eighty-five in 1953.

LEON "GOOSE" GOSLIN

Inducted in 1968 • Years with the Browns 1930–1932

1921–1938	G	AB	R	H	2B	3B	HR	RBI	SB	BB	SO	BA
18 Seasons	2287	8656	1483	2735	500	173	248	1610	89	949	585	.316

It's a good thing that Clark Griffith was an astute baseball man. At least it was for a burly left-handed hitter named Leon Goslin.

As the story goes, Griffith went to scout Goslin in 1920. Goslin wasn't much of a fielder and actually got hit on the head while trying to catch a fly ball. Luckily, he also hit three home runs that day, and Griffith decided Goslin's bat was more powerful than the glove and signed the young power hitter.

All Goslin did after that was lead his major league teams to five World Series appearances, two World Series championships, and drive in 100 runs and hit better than .300 on eleven occasions en route to a .316 lifetime batting average.

Unfortunately, none of those World Series appearances came during the three years he played for the St. Louis Browns.

Leon Allen "Goose" Goslin was born in Salem, New Jersey, where he was raised on a prosperous farm. That hard work helped Goslin gain his strength. But the young Goslin often ignored his farm duties to play baseball. His play eventually earned him a minor league contract.

Goose started out as a pitcher. However, his shrewd manager moved Goslin to the outfield where his everyday hitting drew increased attention—especially from Griffith, who wound up signing Goslin to a $6,000 contract. In spite of his outfield misadventures, he was called up to the majors at the end of the 1921 season.

His difficulty in judging fly balls quickly earned him the nickname Goose by one of the Washington newspapers that wrote: "He often looked like a bird

LEON ALLEN GOSLIN
"GOOSE"
WASHINGTON A.L. 1921 TO 1930, 1933, 1938
ST. LOUIS A.L. 1930 TO 1932
DETROIT A.L. 1934 TO 1937
BATTED .344 IN 1924, .334 IN 1925,
.354 IN 1926, .334 IN 1927. LED A.L.
IN BATTING IN 1928 WITH .379 AVERAGE.
RUNS BATTED IN FOR 1924-129.
HIT .300 OR BETTER 11 YEARS.
LIFETIME TOTAL OF 2735 HITS,
BATTING AVERAGE .316.
MADE 37 HITS IN 5 WORLD SERIES.

flapping its wings when he chased the ball." His long neck and ample nose added to the nickname that he'd carry for the rest of his life.

His hitting, however, was never a point of ridicule.

In his first full season with Washington in 1922, Goose hit .324 and followed that up two years later by leading the American League with 129 RBIs while hitting .344. His 12 home runs (remember, this was the dead-ball era) set a single-season team record. He shattered that with 18 homers the next year and hit three more homers in the Senators' second consecutive World Series.

In 1926 Goslin led Washington with a .354 average while hitting 17 homers—all on the road—the most ever by a player who didn't hit any at home.

Goslin finally won his only batting title in '28, hitting .379. However, he also suffered an arm injury and his stats fell way off in 1929 when he hit only .288.

Another factor may have been his feud with new manager Walter Johnson, which led to a trade early in 1930 that sent Goslin to the Browns for Heine Manush. In those three years in St. Louis, Goslin's bat exploded with 30 home runs in 1930 (he also hit seven for Washington before the trade), 24 in 1931, and 17 in 1932, while driving in more than 100 runs each year.

After the '32 season, Goslin was traded back to Washington, where he spent a year before being dealt to Detroit. He played in Detroit until 1937, finishing his career briefly in 1938, again with Washington.

1924–1935, 1937	G	AB	R	H	2B	3B	HR	RBI	SB	BB	BA
13 Seasons	1283	4625	777	1466	341	67	164	833	70	372	.317

It would be hard to imagine just how great a baseball player Chick Hafey could have been if he played healthy and had decent eyesight. As it was, the bespectacled outfielder was still one of the best of his era. John McGraw, one of the top field generals of the early 1900s, called Hafey one of the best of his generation.

Charles James "Chick" Hafey was bothered most of his career with a sinus condition that weakened him to the extent that he averaged less than one hundred games a year during his thirteen seasons in the major leagues. In addition, during the 1926 season, Hafey was beaned on four different occasions and continually complained of headaches and deteriorating eyesight. Those maladies, however, didn't prevent him from winning the National League batting title in 1931 and finishing among the leaders in homers six times en route to the Hall of Fame.

The line drive hitting, strong-armed Hafey actually came to the attention of the Cardinals as a pitching prospect, but after seeing his hitting prowess in the minor leagues, general manager Branch Rickey converted him to an outfielder.

CHARLES JAMES HAFEY
"CHICK"
ST. LOUIS N.L. 1924-1931
CINCINNATI N.L. 1932-1937
GREAT OUTFIELDER WHO COMPILED .317 LIFETIME BATTING AVERAGE. LEADING HITTER OF N.L. WITH .349 IN 1931. BATTED .329 OR BETTER SIX CONSECUTIVE YEARS. EQUALLED LEAGUE RECORD OF TEN HITS IN SUCCESSION, 1929. LIFETIME FIELDING AVERAGE .971.

Hafey was so talented that at one point, slugging teammate Rogers Hornsby called him "the best right-handed hitter I ever saw." And who could dispute that statement from the person whom many consider to be the best right-handed hitter to play baseball. Hornsby also noted that Hafey would have hit more home runs (his high was 29) if his line drive style took on a more uppercut direction. Still, he averaged 27 home runs and 114 RBIs from 1928 to 1930.

With two good eyes, Hafey may have been even better. His eyesight seemed to deteriorate after the 1926 beanings. Team surgeon Dr. Robert F. Hyland and his teammates also became aware of a decline in his eyesight, noticing he couldn't see the red "exit" sign in their Pullman car. Hyland diagnosed Hafey with the sinus problem and convinced him to wear glasses, making him the first baseball star to wear them on a regular basis in the twentieth century. (Specs Toporcer was the first baseball player to wear glasses, but Hafey was the most prominent.) Actually, Hafey's eyesight fluctuated to the point that he alternated between three pairs of glasses.

ST. LOUIS CARDINALS

Hafey's efforts in 1931 helped the Cardinals capture the World Series title. However, the season started slowly for him. A contract dispute and his constant sinus problems plagued him, and through June 4 he had only 65 plate appearances. Hafey got back in the batting race and on August 19 went 3 for 3 and took over the lead for the first time with a .347 average. Actually, it all boiled down to Hafey's last at-bat—a single that gave him a final .3489 average to Bill Terry's .3486 and Bottomley's .3482.

Prior to the start of that season, Hafey held out over a contract dispute. He had little salary increases leading up to the 1931 season and wanted $15,000 to play. He signed for $12,500 just prior to the start of the season. But Rickey, demanding that he prove he was fit to play, sent Hafey to the Cardinals' Danville affiliate and then kept him on the bench for the first few weeks of the season and fined him

$2,400. Proving his point, Hafey won the batting title and helped the Redbirds win the World Series crown.

In 1932, coming off his batting title, Hafey was still upset about the previous year's fine and wanted that amount added to his 1932 salary. Rickey refused, and instead of again acquiescing to the general manager, Hafey left spring training. Getting in the last lick, Rickey's answer was to trade him to the last-place Cincinnati Reds on opening day. The trade was also prompted by the presence of a youngster named Joe Medwick.

Hafey got his raise from Cincinnati, but his vision was still erratic and, coupled with his sinus condition, he lost half of the 1932 season, playing in only 83 games. Still, he finished with a .344 average. In 1933 he was chosen for the inaugural All-Star Game, recording the first-ever All-Star hit, a single in the second inning.

He finished his career with a .317 average, 164 home runs, and 833 runs batted in. Hafey played in four World Series for the Cardinals in 1926, 1928, 1930, and 1931. Helped in large part by former teammate Frankie Frisch's recommendation, he was elected to the Hall of Fame in 1971.

186—Sportsman's Park, St. Louis, Missouri

"CHICK"
HAFEY

HENRY "HEINE" MANUSH

Inducted in 1964 • Years with the Browns 1928–1930

1923–1939	G	AB	R	H	2B	3B	HR	RBI	SB	BB	SO	BA
17 Seasons	2008	7654	1287	2524	491	160	110	1183	113	506	345	.330

He spent only a little more than two of his 17 major league seasons with the St. Louis Browns, but that was all the St. Louis fans needed to see why Heine Manush was called the Hitting Machine.

Born Henry Emmett Manush, the left-handed hitting outfielder was always among the top hitters in the major leagues. He twice hit .378 and earned one American League batting title and finished second on two other occasions, en route to a .330 lifetime batting average.

In 1926, while with the Detroit Tigers, Manush collected six hits in a final-day, season-ending doubleheader to finish at .378, edging the New York Yankees' Babe Ruth for the batting championship. Two years later, his first season with the Browns, he again hit .378, but lost the batting title to Goose Goslin, for whom he was later traded, by a single point.

In 1933, with the Washington Senators, he finished second to Jimmie Foxx in the batting race with a .336 average, but his league-leading 221 hits and 17 triples paced the Senators to a pennant.

HENRY EMMET MANUSH
1923–1939
SLUGGING OUTFIELDER
FOR 6 MAJOR LEAGUE CLUBS. BATTING
CHAMPION OF A.L. AT .378 WITH 1926 TIGERS.
LIFETIME AVERAGE OF .330 IN 2,009
MAJOR LEAGUE GAMES. HAD 2,524 HITS.

He was selected for Major League Baseball's second-ever All-Star Game in '34. But while he let his bat do the talking, he allowed his temper to get in the way on occasion.

Manush was born to German parents (hence the nickname Heine) in Tuscumbia, Alabama, in 1901. He was one of seven sons, six of whom ended up playing professional baseball. In 1920, just before his nineteenth birthday, he began his professional career with Portland in the Western League. Two years later, he hit .376 with 20 homers and was signed as a free agent with the Detroit Tigers.

The promotion to the majors was doubly exciting for Manush since his older brother, Frank, was already in the big leagues, playing third base for the Philadelphia Athletics.

During his rookie season, Manush hit .334 while playing in an outfield alongside future Hall of Famers Ty Cobb and Harry Heilmann, forming what many have called the finest outfield in baseball history. Manush also benefited from Cobb's knowledge of hitting. Cobb reportedly urged his young protégé to choke up on the bat, to shorten his swing and "go with the pitch,"

79

instead of trying to pull the ball.

Manush played five seasons with Detroit, but following the 1927 season (after Cobb had departed Detroit and coupled with disagreements with the Tigers' manager) Detroit traded him to the Browns.

That first season in St. Louis, Manush led the league with 241 base hits en route to that .378 average. Included were a league-leading 47 doubles, a club-record-tying 20 triples, 13 home runs, and 108 runs batted in. He finished second to the New York Yankees' Mickey Cochran in the hotly contested Most Valuable Player voting.

Some 49 games into the 1930 season, he was traded to Washington in exchange for Goslin, the player who barely beat him out of the batting title in 1928. During those 2½ seasons with the Browns, in which he played in 345 games, Manush collected 510 hits, including 108 doubles, while posting a .362 average.

Manush went on to play six seasons with the Senators, leading the league with 221 hits and 17 triples in 1933. That was also the year Manush played in his only World Series (the Senators lost in five games to the New York Giants). However, he didn't fare too well in that series, and letting his temper get the best of him, took it out on the umpires.

According to a Society for American Baseball Research report, in Game 3 the Senators had the tying run on second with two out in the sixth inning. Manush hit a ball that first baseman Howie Critz somehow grabbed and flipped to pitcher Carl Hubbell to nip Manush—at least that was according to umpire Charlie Moran. An infuriated Manush hotly debated the call. The home

During his rookie season, Manush hit .334 while playing in an outfield alongside future Hall of Famers Ty Cobb and Harry Heilmann, forming what many have called the finest outfield in baseball history.

plate umpire finally broke up the fierce argument. But Manush gave Moran one more verbal blast on his way out to right field and was tossed from the game. Manush had to be physically restrained from the first base umpire. Manush recalled the play years later. "It actually was more than an argument," he said. "Moran had every right to chase me . . . But when he bellied up to me and asked me what I wanted to make of it, there was a temptation that was too great. Moran, like the other umps in those days, was wearing a black bow tie, the kind that comes with an elastic band. What I did was grab the tie and let it snap back into Moran's neck. That's when he gave it to me."

Commissioner Kenesaw Mountain Landis, who was at the game, ruled from then on that no player in the World Series could be thrown out without first getting the commissioner's permission.

Manush finished his career playing one year with the Boston Red Sox, then parts of two seasons with the Brooklyn Dodgers and two brief stints with the Pittsburgh Pirates.

He retired at thirty-seven after the 1939 season. During his career, he had four 200-hit seasons, 40 doubles five times, and a .330 career average. He was inducted into the Hall of Fame by the Veterans Committee in 1964.

1932–1948	G	AB	R	H	2B	3B	HR	RBI	SB	BB	BA
17 Seasons	1984	7635	1198	2471	540	113	295	1383	42	437	.324

Outspoken, opinionated, and downright cantankerous, Joseph Michael Medwick knew how to play baseball, and he became a charter member of the St. Louis Cardinals' famed Gashouse Gang with his aggressive style. Nicknamed Ducky because of the way he walked, the strapping outfielder joined the Cardinals in 1932 and starred for them until he was traded to the Brooklyn Dodgers in 1940.

He won both the Most Valuable Player Award and the Triple Crown in 1937 by leading the National League in batting average (.374), home runs (31), and runs batted in (154). He compiled career highs that season not only in the Triple Crown categories, but also in hits, slugging percentage, on-base percentage, and total bases. No National League player has won the Triple Crown since. During his MVP season, he also led the league with 111 runs, 237 hits, and 56 doubles. In fact, Medwick continues to hold the major league record with seven consecutive seasons of 40 or more doubles, a mark he set between the 1933 and 1939 campaigns. His MVP season came on the heels of another

JOSEPH MICHAEL MEDWICK
"DUCKY WUCKY"

ST. LOUIS N.L. 1932 TO 1940, 1947, 1948
BROOKLYN N.L. 1940 TO 1943, 1946
NEW YORK N.L. 1943 TO 1945 – BOSTON N.L. 1945

LED N.L. IN BATTING IN 1937 WITH .374
AVERAGE. BATTED .353 IN 1935, .351 IN 1936,
.332 IN 1939. LIFETIME TOTAL 2471 HITS.
BATTING AVERAGE .324. NAMED TO ALL STAR
TEAMS 1935-6-7-8-9. MOST VALUABLE PLAYER
N.L. 1937. LED N.L. IN RUNS BATTED IN
AND TWO BASE HITS 1936-7-8.
BATTED .300 OR MORE 15 TIMES.

great campaign in 1936 when he led the league with 223 hits, 64 doubles, and 138 RBIs. The 64 doubles tied George Burns's record for the most ever hit by a right-handed batter. A ten-time All-Star, he played for seventeen years, finishing with a lifetime .324 batting average. He also drove in and scored 100 runs six times.

Medwick also has another claim to fame—he is the only player ever taken off the field during a World Series game. In Game 7 of the 1934 series against Detroit, Medwick tripled into deep center and slid hard into Tiger third baseman Marv Owen in the top of the eighth inning. When he took the field in the bottom half of the inning, Tigers fans showered the field with garbage, most of it aimed at Medwick in left field. Commissioner Kenesaw Mountain Landis removed Medwick from the game for his own safety, with the Cardinals leading 9–0. Years later, Owen reportedly was asked whether Medwick had slid in to hurt him. "No, it was my fault. I was on the bag, faking as if the throw was coming to me, and Joe did what any good runner would do. It was not his fault."

Medwick was traded to the Brooklyn Dodgers during the 1940 season for three players and $125,000 in cash. He helped lead the Dodgers to a pennant in 1941 but had lost much of his dominance after being nearly killed by a beanball thrown at him by former Cardinal teammate Bob Bowman six days after his 1940 trade. He eventually returned to finish his career with the Cardinals in 1947 and 1948.

During a USO tour by a number of players in 1944, Medwick was among several individuals given an audience by Pope Pius XII. Upon being asked by the pope what his vocation was, Medwick replied,

"Your Holiness, I'm Joe Medwick. I, too, used to be a Cardinal."

In 1963 Medwick was not a member of the Hall of Fame. Never at a loss for words, he commented, "The young writers, they ought to do more homework." Five years later, in 1968, the Veterans Committee elected him to the Hall of Fame.

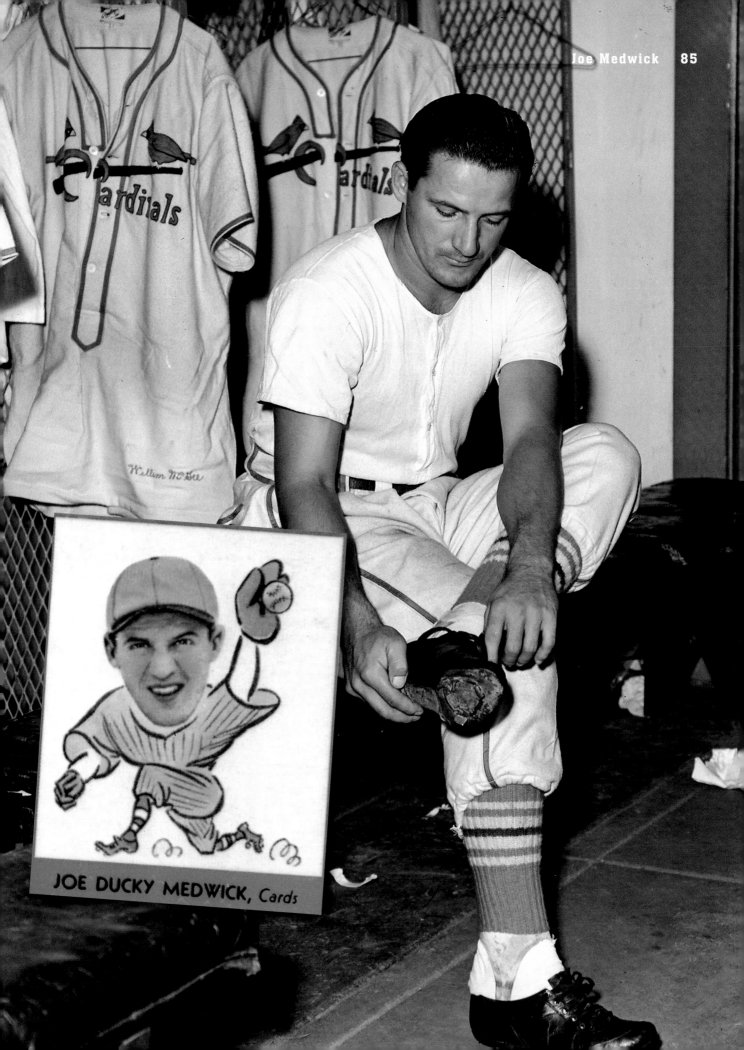

JOE DUCKY MEDWICK, Cards

STAN "THE MAN" MUSIAL

Inducted in 1969 • Years with the Cardinals 1941–1963

1941–1963	G	AB	R	H	2B	3B	HR	RBI	SB	BB	BA
22 Seasons	3026	10,972	1949	3630	725	177	475	1951	78	1599	.331

Stan Musial was simply the greatest Cardinal of them all. His footprint on the history of the Cardinals beginning in 1941 to his last game in 1963 is overwhelming. There were championship seasons and second-division struggles, but in every case there was Musial's unmistakable image as the complete ballplayer, the team leader, and the competitor.

The story is a classic and one many people know. Son of a Polish immigrant, growing up in Donora, Pennsylvania, Stan had to ask his mother to get his father to change his mind and sign a baseball contract for him at age seventeen. Dad wanted his first son to go to college at the University of Pittsburgh, unimpressed by the thought of a career in baseball.

With reluctance, Stan's father signed the agreement, and Stan headed for the St. Louis Cardinals Class D League team as a left-handed pitcher for Williamson, West Virginia, for two seasons—1937 and 1938. He was not impressive and was nearly released when an injury to another player forced him into the lineup as an outfielder. He hit .352, and though Stan continued to pitch into 1940 at Daytona Beach, it was his hitting that was getting attention. A diving catch attempt ended his pitching career and saved his major league career!

He was a spark in September 1941. He played in just twelve big league games, after jumping from Class C to Class B to St. Louis. He had 6 hits in a doubleheader and a total of 20 hits, 7 RBIs, and a .426 batting average for St. Louis. The effort was enough to earn a shot for the 1942 Cardinals outfield. He became the youngest player on a championship team. His first hit of the World Series drove in the winning run of Game 2, preventing the Yankees from going up 2–0.

Stan never met a team he couldn't hit against, but he would admit to a special relationship between himself and the Brooklyn Dodgers. He "murdered the Bums" on a regular basis. His success caused Dodger fans to fear his every at-bat, with a .356 career batting average at Ebbets Field. As the story goes, those fans of the Bums were the ones who dubbed our hero the Man. In 1946 when Stan approached the plate in a tight situation, the fans cringed and some were heard to say, "Oh no, here comes the Man again!"

STANLEY FRANK MUSIAL
"THE MAN"
ST. LOUIS CARDINALS 1941-1963

HOLDS MANY NATIONAL LEAGUE RECORDS, AMONG THEM: GAMES PLAYED 3,026; AT BATS 10,972; HITS 3,630; MOST RUNS SCORED 1,949; MOST RUNS BATTED IN 1951; TOTAL BASES 6,134. LED N.L. IN TOTAL BASES 6 YEARS AND WON SEVEN N.L. BATTING TITLES. MOST VALUABLE PLAYER 1943, 1946, 1948. PLAYED IN 24 ALL-STAR GAMES. LIFETIME BATTING AVERAGE .331.

Musial broke out in 1943 as the Cardinals' offensive leader. The year marked his first All-Star Game and his first National League Most Valuable Player Award in another pennant-winning season.

Stan the Man had the "peek-a-boo" stance, as he peered menacingly over his right shoulder, feet close together in the left-hander's side of the batter's box.

His statistics gave him the top spot in six different offensive categories: 220 hits, 48 doubles, 20 triples, 347 total bases, a .425 on-base percentage, and a .562 slugging percentage. Only this time, the Cardinals, who had won the NL pennant by a giant eighteen games, ended up losing the World Series.

The gap in Stan's career that left him 25 homers short of 500 was his military duty in 1945. Actually, he was fortunate not to miss 1944 as well, but despite having taken the physical, he was left alone to hit .347 with 197 hits, 12 homers, and 94 runs batted in. That was the Streetcar Series with the St. Louis Browns, won by Stan's Birds four games to two.

A turning point in the Musial legend occurred in 1946 when he resisted big cash—$125,000 a year for five years and a $50,000 bonus—to leave the country to play in Mexico, which some stars of the game did. Stan refused the money, opting instead for $13,500 before getting

a "thank you" $5,000 raise. Now a first baseman, he smashed 228 hits, 50 doubles, 20 triples, for a .365 league-leading average, with 124 runs, a .587 slugging percentage, 103 RBIs, and 16 homers. They wheeled up to his front door a second MVP trophy. The 1946 pennant and championship would be Stan's last as a player.

As if he hadn't done enough, Stan the Man went on a barrage at the plate from 1948, when he almost won the Triple Crown, through 1955. The 1948 campaign, another near miss for the ball club, was a giant one for Musial. In late June he was hitting .408, which led Brooklyn pitcher Preacher Roe to quip, "My new strategy with Musial will be to walk him and then pick him off first base!" Musial led the league in almost everything that season—a .376 batting average, 230 hits, 46 doubles, 18 triples, 429 total bases, and a .702 slugging percentage. The 138-point margin in the slugging percentage was the National League's largest since 1925. His 131 RBIs also led the NL, but sadly, a rainout in which Musial homered cost him the Triple Crown. He did win his third MVP, the most by any National Leaguer.

Stan the Man had the "peek-a-boo" stance, as he peered menacingly over his right shoulder, feet close together in the left-hander's side of the batter's box. He would uncoil his body and use his legs to drive the ball to all parts of the field. There was a special day on May 2, 1954, at Busch Stadium against the New York Giants. After walking the first time up, the Man cranked a Johnny Antonelli pitch on the pavilion roof for a home run. In the fifth inning he duplicated the feat, same place. He singled in the sixth only to belt another dinger in the eighth, and it proved to be the game-winner in a 9–6 finish. In the second game of the doubleheader, he hit his longest blast, dead center to the wall where the Giants' young star Willie Mays caught it at the 402 mark. Later, against Hall of Fame knuckleballer Hoyt Wilhelm, Stan knocked two more over the pavilion roof for five home runs in a doubleheader—a major league record later tied by San Diego's Nate Colbert in 1972.

A lot of highlights happen in a twenty-two-year career. In the 1955 All-Star Game, Stan entered the game in the fourth inning, went on to play left field right through the twelfth inning when he hit a walk-off homer, earning a 6–5 National League win. He recorded his 3,000th base hit at Wrigley Field on May 13, 1958, a ringing double into left field.

He played left field in his younger days. Then, as time went on and age became a factor, he did not hesitate to take the team's suggestion of moving to first base. Stan was such an honest guy as well. After his 1959 season, where he slumped to .255 in 115 games, he asked for and was granted a pay cut from $100,000 to $75,000.

Musial's records at the time of retirement were staggering. He held or tied seventeen major league records, twenty-nine National League records, and nine All-Star Game records. What speaks for his

In 1955 Musial poses with the bat he used to hit his 300th career home run.

character is a squeaky-clean record of having never been ejected from a major league game, some 3,026.

His lifetime totals of hits, runs, and at-bats were second only to Ty Cobb at retirement. His RBI total was fourth all-time, and only Hank Aaron surpassed his extra base hit total of 1,477. Today, he still stands fourth in total hits behind Pete Rose, Ty Cobb, and Hank Aaron. He has that incredible mark of consistency—1,815 hits on the road and 1,815 hits at home!

His No. 6 uniform was the first number retired in the great history of Cardinals baseball. Future Hall of Fame broadcaster Bob Costas said it all when he described Stan Musial as a man who "represents more than two decades of sustained excellence and complete decency as a human being."

He continued to serve after retiring as a player. He was President Lyndon Johnson's national physical fitness adviser; he was the Cardinals general manager for a championship season; and he owned a restaurant in St. Louis. Musial had a statue erected in his honor at Busch Stadium and was elected to the Baseball Hall of Fame in 1969, being named on 93 percent of the ballots in his first year of eligibility. He ranked tenth on the *Sporting News*'s list of the one hundred greatest players, was honored as one of the thirty players on the All-Century Team, was inducted into the Hall of Famous Missourians, the Missouri Sports Hall of Fame, and the St. Louis Sports Hall of Fame in 2009.

Oh yes, and he wouldn't want it forgotten that he recorded eighteen songs on his harmonica, performed on the TV show *Hee Haw*, and had his very own *Stan Musial Harmonica Instruction Book*.

MUSIAL RAPS OUT 3,000th HIT

BASEBALL THRILLS

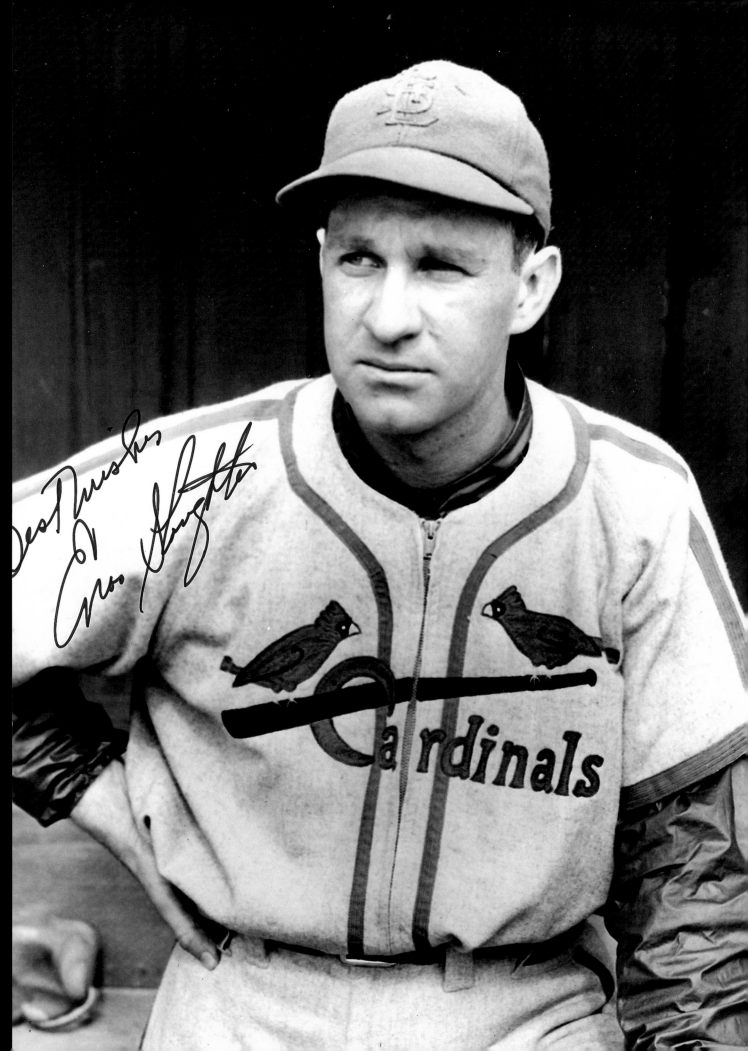

1938–1942, 1946–1959	G	AB	R	H	2B	3B	HR	RBI	SB	BB	BA
19 Seasons	2383	7946	1247	2383	413	148	169	1304	71	1018	.300

When the Cardinals needed a new shining light to come along in 1938 as the glow was fading on the Gashouse Gang, along came a country boy from North Carolina. Enos Slaughter brought with him the hustling spirit that typified the Gashouse Gang while adding another dimension to the birds on the bat. He ran like the wind, hit like the devil, and played the game as hard as anyone who ever wore the uniform. He was hungry for success, and yet off the field, he was the Southern gentleman.

After a .276 batting average his rookie season, the left-handed hitting outfielder began a string of five straight seasons and seven of eight consecutive years of hitting more than .300. Interrupting that streak were three years in which he served in the Armed Forces (1943–1945).

After his freshman season at age twenty-two, Enos and his father, Zadok, had gone rabbit hunting and came home to eat their spoils. Unbeknownst to them, the rabbits were infected, and with few medical options available, Zadok died the same night and Enos came close to death. He would suffer emotional and physical problems into his second season, but the gutty right fielder came through for his team, hitting .320 with 86 RBIs and a league-leading 52 doubles.

Slaughter became a staple in the outfield. His .318 in 1942 was second best in the NL. Some think the Cardinals outfield beginning in 1942 was the team's best ever, with Stan Musial in left, Terry Moore in center, and Slaughter in right. Only his teammate, catcher Walker Cooper, garnered more votes for the NL MVP Award in 1942 when Slaughter had 100 runs scored, 31 doubles, 17 triples, 13 home runs, 98 RBIs, 88 walks, and a .412 on-base percentage.

Enos won four world championships, two with the Cardinals and two later with the New York Yankees. His first in 1942 was a four-game sweep that shocked the favored Yankees. The win in 1946 is where Slaughter played a pivotal role. In the deciding Game 7, he was on first base with a single in the bottom of the eighth inning with two outs and Harry "the Hat" Walker at the plate. Slaughter had made up his mind. He was running on the pitch to Walker, who slashed the baseball

ENOS BRADSHER SLAUGHTER
"COUNTRY"
ST. LOUIS N.L. 1938-1953
NEW YORK A.L. 1954-1955, 1956-1959
KANSAS CITY A.L. 1955-1956 MILWAUKEE N.L. 1959
HARD-NOSED, HUSTLING PERFORMER WHO PLAYED
THE GAME WITH INTENSITY AND DETERMINATION.
FLAT, LEVEL SWING MADE HIM A LIFETIME .300
HITTER WHO INVARIABLY CAME THROUGH IN
CLUTCH SITUATIONS. EXCELLENT OUTFIELDER WITH
STRONG ARM. DARING BASERUNNER FAMOUS FOR
HIS MAD DASH HOME TO WIN 1946 WORLD SERIES
FOR CARDINALS. BATTED .291 IN 5 WORLD SERIES.

into left-center field. Slaughter had a good shot of reaching third base. However, with the game on the line and Boston having just scored two game-tying

His daring style, his speed on the bases and in the field, and his trademark run to first base all the time, whether it was a single or walk, set him apart.

runs, Enos decided to take matters into his own hands. Years later he recalled the moment. "Harry hit one into left center," Slaughter began, "not too hard. I got a good jump and when I got to second and saw in front of me where the ball was going I said to myself, 'I can score.' I kept going. I never broke stride. I had it in my head I was going

to score. Sometimes you just make up your mind about something and everything else gets locked out. I still don't know to this day if our third base coach Mike Gonzales ever gave me the stop sign or not. It wouldn't have made a lick of difference if he had. I rounded third and kept going. When I got ready to slide into home I saw Roy Partee, the catcher, take about two or three steps up in front of the plate and I slid across it easily."

The Red Sox center fielder had fired the ball to shortstop Johnny Pesky, but he couldn't hear above the roar of the crowd the pleas from second baseman Bobby Doerr to throw the ball to home plate. His hesitation gave the Old War Horse, as Slaughter was known, the edge he needed to score. The Cardinals stopped Boston in the ninth and claimed a world championship thanks to Slaughter's "Miracle Dash for Home."

Slaughter, who wore No. 9, was a fan favorite for his extraordinary dedication to the Cardinals. His daring style, his speed on the bases and in the field, and his trademark run to first base all the time, whether it was a single or walk, set him apart.

Overall, "Country" Slaughter hit .300 or better in ten seasons, posted a career average of .300,

ENOS SLAUGHTER
ST. LOUIS CARDINALS – OUTFIELD   1938

HOF · 1985

and finished his career with 2,383 total hits. He was selected for the NL All-Star Team ten times from 1941 to 1953. In Cardinals history he ranks second in RBIs (1,148), third in triples (135), third in walks (839), fourth in games (1,820), fourth in runs (1,071), fourth in hits (2,064), and had eight of his thirteen seasons over .300 in St. Louis. Enos was elected to the Baseball Hall of Fame by the Veterans Committee in 1985.

Enos Slaughter slides home safely after his "mad dash" from first on a single by Harry Walker to score the deciding run in Game 7 of the 1946 World Series.

CHAPTER 4
PITCHERS

GROVER CLEVELAND ALEXANDER

Inducted in 1938 • Years with the Cardinals 1926–1929

1911–1930	W	L	W-L%	ERA	G	GS	CG	SHO	SV	IP
20 Seasons	373	208	.642	2.56	696	600	437	90	32	5190.0

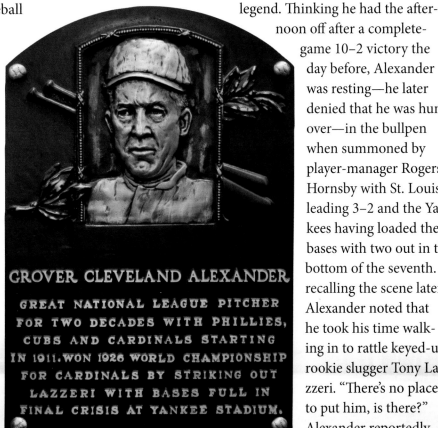

Grover Cleveland Alexander's career is one of the most brilliant yet tragic in baseball history. He won 28 games his first major league season, thus embarking on the route that would lead to the Hall of Fame. But he fought the demons of alcoholism and epilepsy along the way.

A master of the curveball and pinpoint control, Alexander started his professional career in 1909 with Galesburg of the Illinois-Missouri League. He arrived in the majors in 1911 with the Philadelphia Phillies at age twenty-four. That rookie season saw him lead the league with 31 complete games and a 28–13 record. With the Phils he would win 30 or more games in three straight seasons, 1915–1917. In 1916 sixteen of his thirty-three wins were shutouts, tying the record for whitewashings set by George Washington Bradley of the St. Louis Brown Stockings during the NL's charter season in 1876.

Alexander is best remembered by St. Louis fans for his tremendous efforts for the Cardinals in the 1926 World Series against the New York Yankees, led by Babe Ruth and Lou Gehrig.

Alexander, a mid-season acquisition by the Cardinals, won Games 2 and 6, each allowing the Cardinals to tie the series when it looked as if the Yankees would establish their dominance.

But in the seventh game, the pitcher, sometimes dubbed Pete or Alex the Great, became a legend. Thinking he had the afternoon off after a complete-game 10–2 victory the day before, Alexander was resting—he later denied that he was hung over—in the bullpen when summoned by player-manager Rogers Hornsby with St. Louis leading 3–2 and the Yankees having loaded the bases with two out in the bottom of the seventh. In recalling the scene later, Alexander noted that he took his time walking in to rattle keyed-up rookie slugger Tony Lazzeri. "There's no place to put him, is there?" Alexander reportedly told Hornsby when he got to the mound. After Lazzeri cracked a foul ball down the left field line that just missed being a grand slam, Alexander struck him out, getting him to chase the last two pitches, which were just out of the batter's reach on the outside corner.

Alexander then retired the side in order in the eighth and got the first two men in the ninth before walking Babe Ruth. With hard-hitting outfielder Bob Meusel at the plate, Ruth tried to steal second and was gunned out on a perfect throw from catcher Bob O'Farrell to Hornsby.

The following two seasons, Alexander went 21–10 and 16–9 for the Cardinals, helping the team finish a close second to the Pirates in 1927, then win the 1928 pennant. The Yankees, however, battered him in two appearances while sweeping the 1928 series from the Redbirds. Alexander posted a 9–8 record for the Cardinals in 1929, then went 0–3 for the Phillies in 1930 as his major league career concluded.

Alexander was the youngest of thirteen children and played semipro ball in his youth before signing his first professional contract at age twenty-two in 1909 for fifty dollars per month. He had a good first year but received a nearly fatal beaning while playing for Galesburg that left him unconscious for two days. Alexander recovered but suffered double vision for many months. The incident set his career back, but he recovered by 1910, became a star pitcher again, and was sold to the Philadelphia Phillies.

His 1911 season featured a league-leading 28 wins, still a modern-day rookie record, 31 complete games, 367 innings pitched, and seven shutouts,

while he finished second in strikeouts and fourth in ERA. The best, however, was yet to come.

From 1911 to 1920, Alexander led the league in ERA five times, wins six times, innings seven times, strikeouts six times, complete games five times, and shutouts six times. In 1915 he was instrumental in leading the Phillies to their first pennant while hurling a record four one-hitters.

After the 1917 season, the Phillies sold Alexander to the Cubs, fearful that he would be lost to the army in World War I. He indeed was drafted and spent most of the 1918 season in France as an artillery officer, where he suffered from shell shock, partial hearing loss, and increasingly worse seizures. Alexander also hit the bottle particularly hard after the war, some say to ward off the epilepsy attacks.

However, he still managed to lead the league in ERA the next two years with the Cubs, posting a 1.72 in 1919, when he was 16–11, and a 1.91 in 1920, when he led in victories with 27.

With the advent of the livelier baseball in the 1920s, Alexander no longer put up high strikeout numbers or earned run averages below 2.00; however, his walks, already low, dropped even more, and he won more than twenty games in two seasons while maintaining an ERA below the league average. After the 1925 season, he entered a sanatorium and in 1926 was suspended by Cubs manager Joe McCarthy, who

Mathewson for the NL career record. Alexander lost 208 games, attaining a losing record only in his final season. He holds NL records for most complete games with 437 and shutouts with 90. He struck out 2,199 hitters while walking only 953 in 5,190 innings.

He was selected to the Hall of Fame in 1938, the first year for the Hall of Fame ceremonies.

Alexander is best remembered by St. Louis fans for his tremendous efforts for the Cardinals in the 1926 World Series against the New York Yankees, led by Babe Ruth and Lou Gehrig.

considered Alexander's drinking a bad influence on younger players. In June he was put on waivers, and the Cardinals claimed him. He went 9–7 for the Cardinals, helping them win the NL pennant.

Alexander's 373 victories tied him with Christy

MORDECAI "THREE FINGER" BROWN

Inducted in 1949 • Year with the Cardinals 1903

1903–1916	W	L	W-L%	ERA	G	GS	CG	SHO	SV	IP
14 Seasons	239	130	.648	2.06	481	332	271	55	49	3172.1

Sometimes a person can turn a handicap into an advantage that can change his life. That's what happened to Mordecai "Three Finger" Brown, who lost the use of two fingers of his right hand in a corn shredder accident when he was only seven years old. Brown turned that misfortune into one of the finest major league pitching careers of the early twentieth century. He began his big league career with the Cardinals but was traded after one year and became the ace right-hander of the great Chicago Cub teams that won NL pennants from 1906 to 1908 and again in 1910. But twenty years before that, no one gave him much of a chance to do much of anything, especially right-handed.

Mordecai Peter Centennial Brown grew up in the farming town of Nyesville, Indiana, with seven siblings. His love of baseball helped him persevere through his handicap. He found that when he gripped the ball with his reconfigured hand, the ball sailed in on hitters, much like a forkball today, and gave him an excellent curveball, which Ty Cobb called "the most devastating" he had ever faced.

The Cardinals purchased Brown in 1903 from Omaha in the Western League, where reporters started calling him Three Finger. He immediately made an impression in the big leagues. He started twenty-four games his rookie season, posting a 9–13 record with a 2.60 ERA.

While his nine victories as a rookie was not impressive, it should be noted that St. Louis was the last-place team that year in the National League, 46 1/2 games behind the league-leading Pirates. Brown's earned run average was the lowest on the team at 2.60, and his nine wins tied him for most on the team. In December 1903 he was traded to the Cubs for Larry McLean and Jack Taylor, a deal the Cardinals later regretted. Brown played for the Cubs for the next ten years, posting a record of 197–103, and finished with a lifetime mark of 239–130. His battles with the New York Giants' Christy Mathewson epitomized the bitter rivalry between two of the top teams in the era. That rivalry was so bitter that in 1908 Brown reportedly received a half-dozen notes with a clear message: "We'll kill you if you pitch and beat the Giants." A black handprint marked each note, the reported signature of the Italian Mafia. The threats didn't faze Brown, who won two World Series games and didn't allow an earned run in the Cubs defeat of the Detroit Tigers.

In 1906 Brown threw nine shutouts, was 26–6, and had an earned run average of 1.04, the second lowest in the dead-ball era. The Cubs also won the most games in baseball history that year (116), and the pennant. Incredibly durable, Brown pitched in 50 games in 1909 and 53 in 1911. Besides posting a 21–11 record in 1911, he also had 13 saves.

Brown came back to St. Louis with the Federal League Terriers as player-manager in 1914, posting a 12–6 record. He was elected to the Baseball Hall of Fame in 1949.

MORDECAI PETER BROWN
(THREE-FINGERED AND MINER)
MEMBER OF CHICAGO N.L. CHAMPIONSHIP TEAM OF 1906,'07,'08,'10. A RIGHT HANDED PITCHER, WON 239 GAMES DURING MAJOR LEAGUE CAREER THAT ALSO INCLUDED ST. LOUIS AND CINCINNATI N.L. AND CLUBS IN F.L. FIRST MAJOR LEAGUER TO PITCH FOUR CONSECUTIVE SHUTOUTS, ACHIEVING THIS FEAT ON JUNE 13, JUNE 25, JULY 2 AND JULY 4 IN 1908.

1965–1988	W	L	W-L%	ERA	G	GS	CG	SHO	SV	IP
24 Seasons	329	244	.574	3.22	741	709	254	55	2	5217.1

When stubborn resistance rules the day, mistakes are made, and in the case of left-handed pitcher Steve Carlton, perhaps the greatest error in Cardinals history came off the field, not on it. For a few dollars more, "Lefty" might have led the Cardinals to more pennants instead of doing the same for the previously hapless Philadelphia Phillies. Team owner August A. Busch Jr. let anger win over reason and traded Carlton, who had just completed a 20–9 season in 1971, for the Phils' 20-game winner, Rick Wise, who clearly didn't have Lefty's upside.

As a Cardinal from 1965 through 1971, the intimidating 6'4", 210-pound power pitcher with the explosive slider had some roller-coaster seasons. However, he was a key cog on the Bob Gibson–led staff of back-to-back World Series teams in 1967 and 1968. He tied for second on the team in wins with 14 in 1967 and went 13–11 in 1968. In 1969 he followed with a 17–11 campaign, featuring 210 strikeouts and a sterling earned run average of 2.12.

He had become a strikeout artist, and his greatest feat in that regard came on September 15, 1969, a cold, rainy night at Busch Stadium against the eventual world champion New York Mets. Lefty fanned a record-setting 19 Mets, but the Cards still lost the game 4–3, as Carlton gave up a pair of two-run homers to Ron Swoboda.

In the first season of a two-year contract, Carlton slumped to 10–19 in 1970, to lead the National League in losses, a puzzling result for the Cardinals' hierarchy. Then in the final year of the deal, he bounced back with a sparkling 20–9 season in 1971, being named to the NL All-Star Team and the *Sporting News* NL All-Star Team selected by the players at the end of the season. He had turned a corner and was heading into his prime.

Unfortunately, that's when a salary dispute ended Carlton's tenure in St. Louis. Lefty wanted $75,000 a year and Mr. Busch didn't want to reward back-to-back seasons of 10–19 and 20–9, and offered Carlton $5,000 less. The dispute ended in a trade. Carlton may have been the difference in 1973 and 1974, with the Cards just falling short of the pennant both years. Carlton became the best left-hander in the National League if not all of baseball, racking up

STEVEN NORMAN CARLTON
"LEFTY"
ST. LOUIS, N.L., 1965-1971
PHILADELPHIA, N.L., 1972-1986
SAN FRANCISCO, N.L., 1986
CHICAGO, A.L., 1986
CLEVELAND, A.L., 1987
MINNESOTA, A.L., 1987-1988
EXTREMELY FOCUSED COMPETITOR WITH COMPLETE DEDICATION TO EXCELLENCE. THRIVED ON MOUND BY PHYSICALLY AND MENTALLY CHALLENGING HIMSELF OFF THE FIELD. OUT PITCH WAS HARD, BITING SLIDER. 329 VICTORIES SECOND ONLY TO SPAHN AMONG LEFTIES AND 4,136 STRIKEOUTS EXCEEDED ONLY BY RYAN. SHARES N.L. RECORD WITH 19 STRIKEOUTS IN GAME. SIX 20 WIN SEASONS. ONLY HURLER TO WIN 4 CY YOUNG AWARDS.

four 20-plus-win seasons for the Phils, including 27 victories in 1972, when the Phillies could only muster 59 wins total. He had a 1.97 earned run average with 310 strikeouts, en route to his first of four Cy Young Awards.

As the plaque in Cooperstown reads, Carlton was "an extremely focused competitor with complete dedication to excellence." He won 329 games in his career, second among left-handed pitchers to Milwaukee Braves Hall of Famer Warren Spahn. His 4,136 strikeouts ranks second in baseball history behind Nolan Ryan. His 19 strikeouts in a single game was later tied. His two 20-win years in St. Louis combined with his four in Philly

gave him six in his career. He is the only pitcher in major league history to win four Cy Young Awards. Steve Carlton was admitted to the Baseball Hall of Fame in 1994 on his first ballot.

Carlton celebrates with an excited battery mate, Dave Ricketts, after the pitcher set the NL season strikeout record, September 20, 1967.

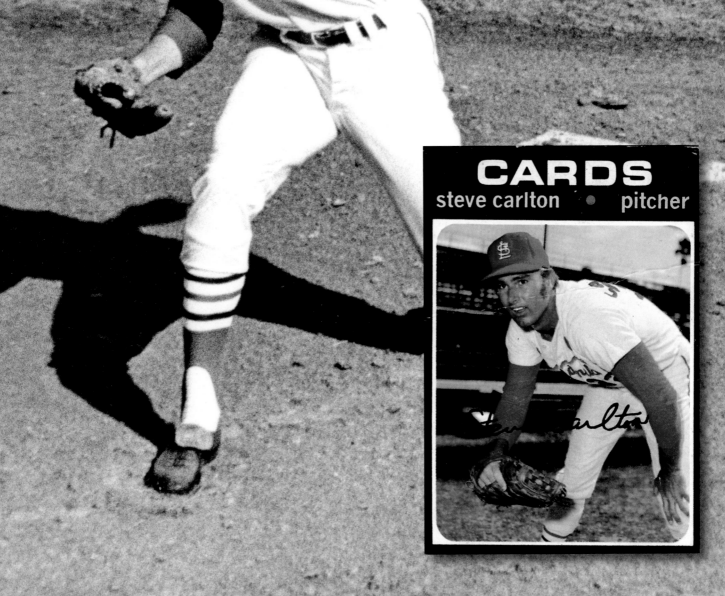

CARDS
steve carlton ● pitcher

1930, 1932–1941	W	L	W-L%	ERA	G	GS	CG	SHO	SV	IP
12 Seasons	150	83	.644	3.02	317	230	154	26	30	1967.1

If there was ever a right time for a baseball player to arrive on the major league scene, especially with the Cardinals, it was Dizzy Dean in the early 1930s. When the Gashouse Gang was in its full glory, Ol' Diz was there to help lead the charge, with his strong right pitching arm on the field and his zaniness off it.

The homespun Hall of Famer, who later turned broadcaster, was the anchor for the Cardinals pitching staff from the time he started in the St. Louis minor league system to the time he was literally knocked off the pitching mound. The injury, a line drive off his toe during the 1937 All-Star Game, came in his sixth full season with the Cardinals and limited the rest of his career to part-time appearances over four years with the Chicago Cubs (and a publicity appearance with the St. Louis Browns in the final game of 1947, for whom he'd been a radio announcer). But those first six seasons were truly marvelous.

Jay Hanna (sometimes know as Jerome Herman) "Dizzy" Dean grew up the son of a poor sharecropper in Lucas, Arkansas, and used to help his father and brother pick cotton.

He dropped out of school by the fourth grade and was pitching for the high school team at age fourteen. The Cardinals signed him at age eighteen in 1929, but he pitched most of his first two seasons in the minor leagues. Dean was called up to the parent club to pitch the last game of 1930—and turned in a three-hit shutout over Pittsburgh. However, the following year he was sent back to Houston, where he led the Texas League with 26 wins, 303 strikeouts, and a 1.57 ERA.

Dean joined the Cardinals for good in 1932 and continued his winning ways, posting 18 victories. He led the NL in strikeouts, shutouts, and innings pitched. But as Ol' Diz liked to say, "You ain't seen nothin' yet." In 1933 he won 20 games and led the league in strikeouts. On July 30, 1933, in the first game of a doubleheader, Dean struck out 17 Chicago Cubs batters to set what was then the record.

From 1933 to 1936, he dominated the league, winning 102 games while losing only 50 times. He led the league in complete games in three of those four seasons, and averaged 50 games and more than 300 innings per season, often coming in from the bullpen between starts. In January 1934 the outspoken Dean boldly predicted the Cardinals would win the NL pennant and that he and his brother Paul would combine to win 45 games that season—an incredible prophecy given that Paul had never pitched a game in the majors. The brothers, however, exceeded that prediction with Dizzy posting a 30–7 record and Paul winning 19. Dizzy led the league in wins, strikeouts, and shutouts, and was second to Carl Hubbell in complete games and ERA. Dean also batted .246. He easily outdistanced Paul Waner for the MVP Award. The Dean brothers each won two games in that year's World Series triumph over the Detroit Tigers.

In 1935 Dean continued on a roll, leading the league for the second straight year, this time with 28 wins. He also led the NL in strikeouts in 1935, for the fourth consecutive year.

Dean also served up plenty of shenanigans, making him one of baseball's premier gate attractions. He gave reporters "exclusives," telling each he had different first and middle names and birthplaces. Once, he even brought a black cat into the stadium and pretended to put a hex on the rival team.

But in 1937 disaster struck Dean and the Cardinals at the All-Star Game. A line drive off the

From 1933 to 1936, he dominated the league, winning 102 games while losing only 50 times.

bat of Cleveland's Earl Averill broke Dean's toe. The injury seemed minor at the time, but the star hurler rushed back too soon, favored his foot, and altered his pitching motion. The result was that he injured his valuable right arm and lost his blazing fastball, finishing the year at 13–10 and logging 197 innings, his lowest total since the 286 he'd hurled in his rookie season.

Dean was traded after the season to the Chicago Cubs, his 7–1 mark and 1.81 ERA in 74 innings helping the Cubs win the 1938 pennant. But Dean would win only six more

Jerome (Dizzy) Dean first played in organized baseball in 1930. Paul (Daffy) Dean in 1931. In 1934 they were largely responsible for bringing the Worlds Championship to The St. Louis Cardinals.

HERE IS JEROME'S FAMOUS CURVE BALL

major league games.

He took his act to the Cardinals broadcast booth in 1941, and the ungrammatical, chatty farm boy was an instant success. For Dean, slide became "slid, slide, slud." Fielders "threwed" the ball, and runners returned to their "respectable" bases. English teachers cringed, but fans roared. He called games for the Cardinals (1941–1946) and then for the Browns. After watching many of the Browns badly pitched games in 1947, Dean reportedly said on the air, "I can pitch better than nine out of the ten guys on this staff!" The Browns management, needing to sell tickets, allowed him to pitch the last game of the season. Dean, then thirty-seven, pitched four innings without allowing a run. After the game, he said of his pitching, "I'm done. Talkin's my game now."

In 1950 Dean began working on the Game of the Week. He lasted as a television and radio broadcaster for two decades and was selected to the Baseball Hall of Fame in 1953.

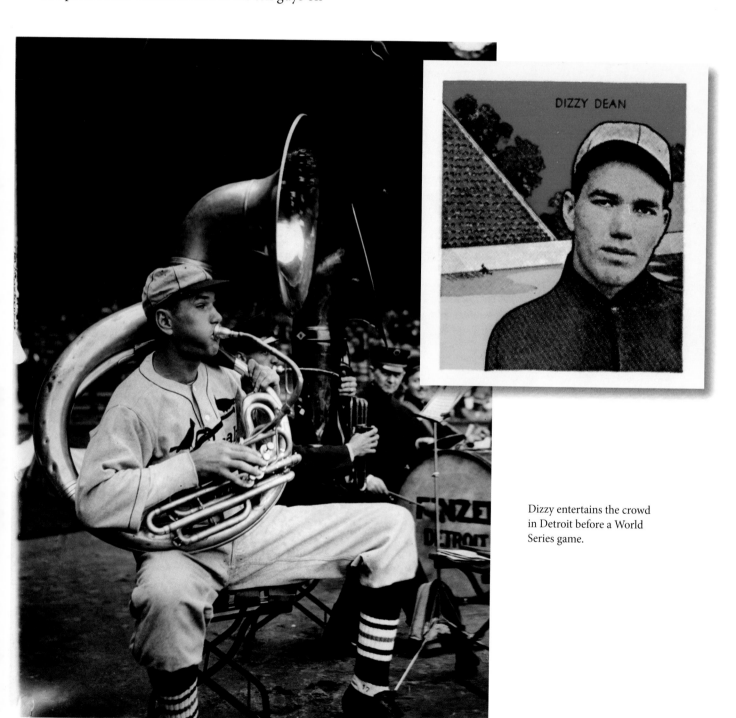

Dizzy entertains the crowd in Detroit before a World Series game.

DENNIS ECKERSLEY

Inducted in 2004 • Years with the Cardinals 1996–1997

1975–1998	W	L	W-L%	ERA	G	GS	CG	SHO	SV	IP
24 Seasons	197	171	.535	3.50	1071	361	100	20	390	3285.2

Dennis Eckersley was young and brash with unstyled, long hair and a fastball clocked at more than ninety miles per hour. In his first twelve seasons, all as a starting pitcher, he averaged almost 13 victories a year, including a 20-win season. But it was his proficiency as a relief pitcher, primarily as a closer, that helped him reach Cooperstown. In fact, he became the first player in major league history to record 100 complete games and 200 saves.

Following a mediocre career as a starter with Cleveland, Boston, and the Chicago Cubs, "Eck" was rejuvenated in 1987 after being traded to the Oakland A's. Tony LaRussa, who had taken over as A's manager the year before, originally sought to use Eckersley as a long reliever–setup man. But the tall right-hander found his niche as a dominant closer when A's regular closer Jay Howell hurt his arm. Eckersley was good, but after abandoning his wild, fireballing style for a more deliberate, pinpoint-control approach, he became spectacular as a closer.

At age thirty-two, when many pitchers are finishing their careers, the flamboyant Eckersley was just beginning his new role as closer. He went on to save 320 games for Oakland, helping the A's to four division titles, three pennants, and a World Series championship. It's no wonder that Eck followed LaRussa and his pitching coach, Dave Duncan, to the Cardinals, helping the Redbirds win the NL Central Division in 1996. In two seasons with the Redbirds, Eck saved 66 games but posted only a 1–11 record.

Eckersley's major league debut season with the Cleveland Indians in 1975 was promising. He went 13–7 with a 2.60 ERA and was named AL Rookie Pitcher of the Year. On May 30, 1977, he hurled a no-hitter against the California Angels, striking out 12. But after that season he was traded to Boston. In his book *The Curse of Rocky Colavito*, Terry Pluto noted that the trade was necessitated by an awkward situation. Eckersley's then-wife, Denise, began a romantic relationship with fellow Indian and, at the time, his best friend, outfielder Rick Manning. Denise and Manning eventually married. The trade seemed to revive Eckersley, who pitched well for Chicago into the mid-1980s, including a 20–8, 2.99 ERA season in 1978. After the 1986 season, he checked himself into a rehabilitation clinic for alcoholism. Cubs officials, unaware of his treatment, traded him to Oakland in early 1987. The renaissance of his career soon followed.

Eckersley dominated the American League in the early and mid-1990s. He gave up just five earned runs in the entire 1990 season, resulting in a microscopic 0.61 ERA. In 1992 he won the AL Cy Young and MVP Awards. Eckersley was elected to the Baseball Hall of Fame in 2004, his first year of eligibility.

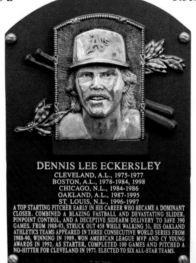

DENNIS LEE ECKERSLEY
CLEVELAND, A.L., 1975-1977
BOSTON, A.L., 1978-1984, 1998
CHICAGO, N.L., 1984-1986
OAKLAND, A.L., 1987-1995
ST. LOUIS, N.L., 1996-1997
A TOP STARTING PITCHER EARLY IN HIS CAREER WHO BECAME A DOMINANT CLOSER. COMBINED A BLAZING FASTBALL AND DEVASTATING SLIDER, PINPOINT CONTROL, AND A DECEPTIVE SIDEARM DELIVERY TO SAVE 390 GAMES. FROM 1988-93, STRUCK OUT 458 WHILE WALKING 51. HIS OAKLAND ATHLETICS TEAMS APPEARED IN THREE CONSECUTIVE WORLD SERIES FROM 1988-90, WINNING IN 1989. WON AMERICAN LEAGUE MVP AND CY YOUNG AWARDS IN 1992. AS STARTER, COMPLETED 100 GAMES AND PITCHED A NO-HITTER FOR CLEVELAND IN 1977. ELECTED TO SIX ALL-STAR TEAMS.

Inducted in 1965 • Year with the Cardinals 1892

1875, 1879–1892	W	L	W-L%	ERA	G	GS	CG	SHO	SV	IP
15 Seasons	365	310	.541	2.85	705	688	646	57	2	6003.1

St. Louis baseball fans may not have heard of James Francis "Pud" Galvin, but he truly represents the founding origins of the Cardinals. Although the pre-1900 era had significant differences from today's game, Pud's pitching statistics are incredible.

A 5'8", 190-pound right-hander with a blistering fastball, Galvin was a pitching giant of his time. He began playing in 1875 with the National Association's St. Louis Reds, but for only one year. His career ended in St. Louis with the Brown Stockings, later to become the Cardinals, in 1892. Between his two St. Louis years, "Pudding" Galvin, so nicknamed because of how he manhandled hitters, jumped around, primarily playing in Pittsburgh and Buffalo. In total, he won 364 games and pitched a whopping 646 complete games.

In his first full season with Buffalo he posted a record of 37–27 and an earned run average of 2.28 in 593 innings over 53 games. Between 1879 and 1884 Galvin had seasons of 37, 20, 28, 28, 46, and 46 victories. In 1880 he lost 35 games with those 20 wins, his only sub-.500 season in that

JAMES F. (PUD) GALVIN
ST. LOUIS N.A. 1875
BUFFALO N.L. 1879-1885
PITTSBURGH A.A. 1885-1886
PITTSBURGH N.L.1887-1889 1891-1892
PITTSBURGH P.L. 1890
ST. LOUIS N.L. 1892
WON 365 GAMES. LOST 311.
WHEN ELECTED ONLY FOUR PITCHERS
HAD WON MORE GAMES.
PITCHED NO-HIT GAMES IN 1880 AND 1884.
PITCHED 649 COMPLETE GAMES.

stretch. He did have the advantage of pitching 45 feet from home plate and later 50 feet, never having to pitch at today's 60 feet, 6 inches.

Pud's 1883 campaign was nothing short of astounding. He went 46–29, had an ERA of 2.72, led the National League with 75 games started, 76 total games pitched, 72 complete games, 656⅓ innings pitched, and five shutouts. He would post 12 shutouts the next season while again winning 46 games, the same year Hoss Radbourn won 60 games!

Galvin joined St. Louis for his final fling and won his last five games, the finale being on August 2, 1892. He has the record for the most 20-win seasons—10—without his team winning a pennant. He hurled two no-hitters over his career. His 6,003 innings pitched and 646 games both stand second in baseball history to the legendary Cy Young, another brief Cardinal Hall of Famer.

Unfortunately he died at the young age of forty-five in Pittsburgh, but he was not forgotten by the Veterans Committee of the Baseball Hall of Fame. Galvin was honored with election in 1965.

BOB GIBSON

Inducted in 1981 • Years with the Cardinals 1959–1975

1959–1975	W	L	W-L%	ERA	G	GS	CG	SHO	SV	IP
17 Seasons	251	174	.591	2.91	528	482	255	56	6	3884.1

His glare was almost as devastating as his ninety-five-mile-per-hour fastball, his scowl was as fearsome as his late-breaking slider. In the mid to late 1960s, he was arguably the best go-to guy when the pressure was most intense.

Bob Gibson, described by many as the fiercest competitor in any baseball era, won 251 games in a 17-year career, all with the St. Louis Cardinals. But he clearly saved his best for the big games. He won seven of his nine World Series starts— eight of them complete games—leading the Redbirds to two World Series championships. Twice he was named MVP of the World Series and is the only pitcher to win a Game 7 and hit a home run in the same contest. In addition, he was the first pitcher to finish his career with more than 3,000 strikeouts since Walter Johnson did so in the 1920s. Gibson also won the Cy Young Award in 1968 and 1970, as well as the NL MVP in 1968.

Nicknamed "Hoot" after the cowboy star with the same last name, Bob Gibson dominated the 1960s. From 1963 to 1970, he won 156 games, an average of 19.5 per season. But his most outstanding accomplishment came during

ROBERT GIBSON
ST. LOUIS N.L., 1959-1975
FIVE-TIME 20-GAME WINNER. HIS 3,117 STRIKEOUTS MADE HIM ONLY 2ND PITCHER TO REACH 3,000. FIRST TO FAN 200 OR MORE IN A SEASON 9 TIMES. SET N.L. MARK WITH 1.12 E.R.A. IN 1968, HURLING 13 SHUTOUTS. TWICE WORLD SERIES MVP, SETTING RECORDS FOR CONSECUTIVE VICTORIES (7), CONSECUTIVE COMPLETE GAMES (8), AND STRIKEOUTS IN A GAME (17) AND A SERIES (35). VOTED N.L. MVP IN 1968 AND CY YOUNG AWARD WINNER IN 1968 AND 1970. WON NINE GOLD GLOVE AWARDS.

1968, and is considered one of the best-ever major league pitching performances. During that season, Gibson went 22–9 with an incredible major league record 1.12 earned run average. That included 13 shutouts, 28 complete games, and a league-leading 268 strikeouts against only 62 walks. Astoundingly, he allowed only 198 hits in 305 innings. During one stretch, he gave up only two runs over 95 consecutive innings in the midst of a 15-game winning streak.

Gibson talked about the Cardinals' lack of run support—a big reason he lost nine games that season— during an interview with *Baseball Digest*: "In '68 I had 13 shutouts and lost five 1–0 games. That's 18 games in which I gave up one run or less. I lost nine games with an ERA of one. How do you do that? It drove me crazy. And people wonder why I was always grumpy."

After that season, termed the Year of the Pitcher, MLB lowered the mound from fifteen to ten inches. The umpires also were instructed to crack down on the inside pitch, one of Gibson's most feared weapons. The change didn't affect

Gibson much, as he went 20–13 with a 2.18 ERA in 1969.

More often than not, Gibby finished what he started, posting 255 career complete games in 482

He signed a minor league contract with the Cardinals and during his first off-season played with the Globetrotters, rooming with one of its stars, Meadowlark Lemon.

starts. In addition, the nimble Gibson won nine consecutive Gold Gloves and hit 24 home runs during his career, five each in the 1965 and 1972 campaigns.

THE WORLD CHAMPIONS
St. Louis
CARDINALS
Bob Gibson
Yearbook 1965

Gibson didn't have it easy growing up as the youngest of seven children in Omaha, Nebraska. His father died of tuberculosis before Bob was born, and his mother had to earn money by doing laundry.

Young Bob, living in Omaha's slums, suffered from asthma, had a heart murmur and rickets, and almost died from pneumonia.

However, as with every other challenge, Gibson overcame his health problems and the slums and went on to star in track, basketball, and baseball in high school. Gibby admitted his first love was basketball, in which he was an all-state player in high school. He attended Creighton University on a basketball scholarship but also played shortstop and outfield in college. During a basketball exhibition against the barnstorming Harlem Globetrotters in 1957, Gibson scored 15 points and later was asked to play with the famous basketball team.

Meanwhile, he'd also caught the eye of the Cardinals, who offered him a four thousand dollar bonus to sign. Still, Gibson was undecided about whether to play basketball or baseball. He signed a minor league contract with the Cardinals and during his first off-season played with the Globetrotters, rooming with one of its stars, Meadowlark Lemon. That was the only season Gibson played pro basketball.

When he reported to the Cardinals' minor league team in Omaha, his manager, Johnny Keane, asked the new outfielder to throw batting practice. Gibson threw so hard, and was just wild enough, that his teammates had trouble hitting him. Keane decided then and there that Gibson was a pitching star of the future. When Keane took over as manager of the Cardinals a few years later, he made Gibson a starter. Later, Gibson noted that it was Keane's confidence in him that changed him from a good pitcher to a great one.

Gibson developed his pitching repertoire, adding a darting slider and a good curve to his already blazing fastball. He struck out 200 batters nine times during his career, and in 1971 struck out 10 in a no-hitter against the Pittsburgh Pirates.

Gibby won 20 games each year from 1965 through 1970, except 1967, when his leg was broken by a line drive off the bat of Roberto Clemente right after the All-Star Game. Gibson returned from the disabled list eight weeks later and went 3–1 with a 0.96 ERA the rest of the regular season. He then starred in the World Series against Boston, allowing only three earned runs and 14 hits while recording three complete-game victories. In fact, Gibby went on to win seven consecutive games and pitched eight straight complete games in World Series competition.

It's no wonder Gibson was elected to the Baseball Hall of Fame in 1981, his first year of eligibility.

Gibson and friend, future Hall of Famer Joe Torre, relax after a game.

BURLEIGH GRIMES

Inducted in 1964 • Years with the Cardinals 1930–1931, 1933–1934

1916–1934	W	L	W-L%	ERA	G	GS	CG	SHO	SV	IP
19 Seasons	270	212	.560	3.53	616	497	314	35	18	4180

Burleigh Grimes was another Hall of Famer who spent a small amount of his career in St. Louis with the Cardinals, but in his case, they were big seasons in Redbird history—1930–1931. St. Louis was 12½ games out of first place with 53 games to play in 1930 when the Birds caught fire. Wild Bill Hallahan would lead the Cardinals staff with 15 wins, but Grimes sizzled with 13 victories and a sparkling 3.02 ERA in a partial season. The Cards took the NL pennant that year but lost in the World Series to the powerful and favored Philadelphia Athletics.

Nicknamed Ol' Stubble-beard, the crafty right-hander molded a 19-year career buoyed by a lively spitball. The pitch wasn't outlawed until 1934. After his playing days, Grimes described his spitball: "I used to chew slippery elm—the bark, right off the tree. Come spring the bark would get nice and loose and you could slice it free without any trouble. What I checked was the fiber from inside, and that's what I put on the ball. That's what they called the foreign substance. The ball would break like hell, away from right-handed hitters and in on lefties."

Whether he was throwing the spitter or not, Burleigh would "show it" by putting both his hands up to his mouth after virtually every pitch. Not surprisingly, Grimes was an irritating opponent. He wore a scowl on the mound and was willing to do what it took to win. Although a gentleman off the field, his temper took over while in uniform. According to some sources, Grimes

BURLEIGH ARLAND GRIMES
1916–1934
ONE OF THE GREAT SPITBALL PITCHERS.
WON 270 GAMES, LOST 212 FOR 7 MAJOR
LEAGUE CLUBS, FIVE 20 VICTORY SEASONS.
WON 13 IN ROW FOR GIANTS IN 1927.
MANAGED DODGERS IN 1937 AND 1938.
LIFETIME E.R.A. 3.52.

actually threw at a batter—in the on-deck circle! That fire was why Frank Frisch wanted Burleigh on his 1930 team despite the running feud between the two players.

Back in 1919, Frisch had apparently spiked Grimes at first base on a close play after a bunt. Swinging fists inevitably followed choice words. Grimes had exacerbated the war with Frisch by throwing in his direction when he thought it necessary in his team's battles with the Cardinals.

When Grimes became a Cardinal, Frisch couldn't have been happier, and they actually became bosom buddies.

The determined Cards roared through the National League in 1931. Grimes rolled to a 17–9 mark, grinding out 217 innings in the 101-win season. As the A's looked for their third straight championship, the Cardinals went to Grimes for Game 7 in the World Series. He battled heroically in the final game, being relieved in the ninth by Hallahan. Grimes garnered the win in the 4–2 victory.

Grimes bounced around over the next few seasons, adding slightly to a resume that ended with 270 wins over 19 seasons. During the 1920s, Grimes had led all pitchers in games started (336), complete games (234), innings (2,798), and wins (190). He played in four World Series—two with the Cardinals, one with Brooklyn in 1920, and finally with the Chicago Cubs in 1932. Grimes was elected to the Baseball Hall of Fame by the Veterans Committee in 1964.

JESSE "POP" HAINES

Inducted in 1970 • Years with the Cardinals 1920–1937

1918, 1920–1937	W	L	W-L%	ERA	G	GS	CG	SHO	SV	IP
19 Seasons	210	158	.571	3.64	555	386	208	24	10	3208.2

From 1920 to 1937, Jesse Haines personified the St. Louis Cardinals. For eighteen seasons, longer than any Cardinals pitcher, Haines relied on a blistering fastball and later a baffling knuckleball en route to 210 victories, the second most to Bob Gibson's 251 victories in team history. Haines's longevity is incredible considering he came to St. Louis when he was twenty-seven years old.

Although the Detroit Tigers signed him, the right-hander played his entire major league career with the Cardinals, except one game, which was his big league debut for the Cincinnati Reds in 1918 when he allowed one run in five innings of work. He was then sent back to the Reds' minor league affiliate. His career turned for the better in 1920 when the Cardinals obtained him from the American Association's Kansas City team, for which he'd gone 21–5 in 1919. In Haines's first full season with the Cardinals, he made a league-high 47 starts and posted a 2.98 ERA, but with a record of 13–20.

He began to pay dividends the following year. Using his fastball, Haines posted an 18–12 mark. Like many pitchers of his day, Haines wasn't averse to knocking down a batter or two who crowded the plate. Haines was a fierce competitor and hated to lose. He was known to glare at his teammates when poor defense cost him a game. Once, he even tore up the Crosley Field clubhouse in Cincinnati after an error cost him a victory. Off the field, however, he was kind and pleasant.

JESSE JOSEPH (POP) HAINES
CINCINNATI N. L. 1918
ST. LOUIS N. L. 1920-1937
DURABLE RIGHT-HANDER WON 210 GAMES,
LOST 158--ALL IN HIS 18 YEARS WITH
CARDINALS. GAINED 20-VICTORY CLASS
THREE TIMES. TOSSED 5-0 NO-HITTER
VS. BOSTON, 1924. DEFEATED YANKEES
TWICE IN 1926 WORLD SERIES, LED N. L.
IN COMPLETE GAMES (25), SHUTOUTS (6)
WHILE POSTING 24-10 RECORD, 1927.

He posted his first 20-win season in 1923 but stumbled to an 8–19 record the next year. One of those 1924 victories, however, was on Tuberculosis Day at Sportsman's Park—a 5–0 no-hitter against Boston on July 17, the first time a St. Louis NL pitcher had thrown a no-hitter since 1876.

Haines later developed a knuckleball, a pitch he learned from Philadelphia's Eddie Rommell. Unlike other pitchers, Haines gripped the ball with his knuckles, rather than the fingertips, allowing his quick-dipping ball to have more speed than other knucklers.

In 1926 Haines posted a 13–4 record to help the Cardinals win the NL pennant. After coming in as a relief pitcher in Game 1, Haines started and shut out the Yankees 4–0 in Game 3, belting a two-run homer to help his own cause. He also started the seventh game and allowed only two runs through six innings. But he developed a blister from throwing his knuckler and in the seventh inning he loaded the bases with two outs. Grover Cleveland Alexander relieved him and struck out New York's Tony Lazzeri for one of the great moments in series history. Haines garnered the Game 7 win.

"Pop" pitched for three more pennant winners: 1930, 1931, and 1934. His record in World Series play was 3–1, with a miserly 1.67 ERA. He also hit .444 with a home run and three RBIs in series play.

Haines posted a career record of 210–158 for the Cardinals and was voted into the Hall of Fame in 1970 by the Veterans Committee.

KID NICHOLS

Inducted in 1949 • Years with the Cardinals 1904–1905

1890–1906	W	L	W-L%	ERA	G	GS	CG	SHO	SV	IP
15 Seasons	361	208	.634	2.95	620	561	531	48	17	5056.1

By the time "Kid" Nichols was hired by the St. Louis Cardinals in 1904, he was well past his prime as a major league pitcher. In fact, he had been gone from the major leagues for a couple of years but decided to take the mound again as player-manager of the team to see if he still had big league stuff. All Nichols did was post a 21–12 record and 2.02 earned run average that year. Not bad for a guy who came out of retirement.

Charles Augustus "Kid" Nichols entered the majors as a brash twenty-year-old in 1890 with the Boston Beaneaters, posting a 27–9 record and a league-leading seven shutouts. In an era when pitchers were expected to go the distance, Nichols went the extra mile. His durability was apparent from his very first season when he hurled 424 innings—unthinkable by today's standards. Over the next three years, he put together records of 30–17, 35–16, 34–14, and 32–13, with 400-plus innings each season.

After winning "only" 26 games in 1895, he went on to lead the league in victories the next

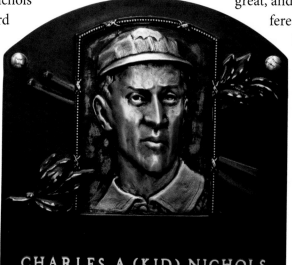

CHARLES A. (KID) NICHOLS
RIGHT HANDED PITCHER WHO WON 30 OR MORE GAMES FOR SEVEN CONSECUTIVE YEARS (1891-97) AND WON AT LEAST 20 GAMES FOR TEN CONSECUTIVE SEASONS (1890-99) WITH BOSTON N.L. ALSO PITCHED FOR ST. LOUIS AND PHILADELPHIA N.L. ONE OF FEW PITCHERS TO WIN MORE THAN 300 GAMES, HIS MAJOR LEAGUE RECORD BEING 360 VICTORIES, 202 DEFEATS.

three years when he won 30, 31, and 31 games. If you're counting, that's seven 30-victory seasons in eight years.

After the 1901 season, Nichols left the majors and purchased a share of a Kansas City minor league team. However, the lure of the majors was great, and when the Cardinals offered him an opportunity to be their player-manager in 1904, he jumped at the chance. Nichols earned two of his 21 victories in the 1904 season in the same day, and he started—and completed!—both games. However, his club finished fifth in the league, and when the Redbirds got off to an even worse start (5–9) in 1905, he was released.

Overall, in fourteen-plus seasons, the right-hander used his overpowering fastball and excellent control to post a 361–208 major league record, with 48 shutouts and a 2.95 ERA. His victory total ranks him seventh all-time. He was a part of five National League championship teams, all with the Boston Beaneaters (1891–1893, 1897–1898).

Nichols was inducted into the Baseball Hall of Fame by the Old Timers Committee in 1949.

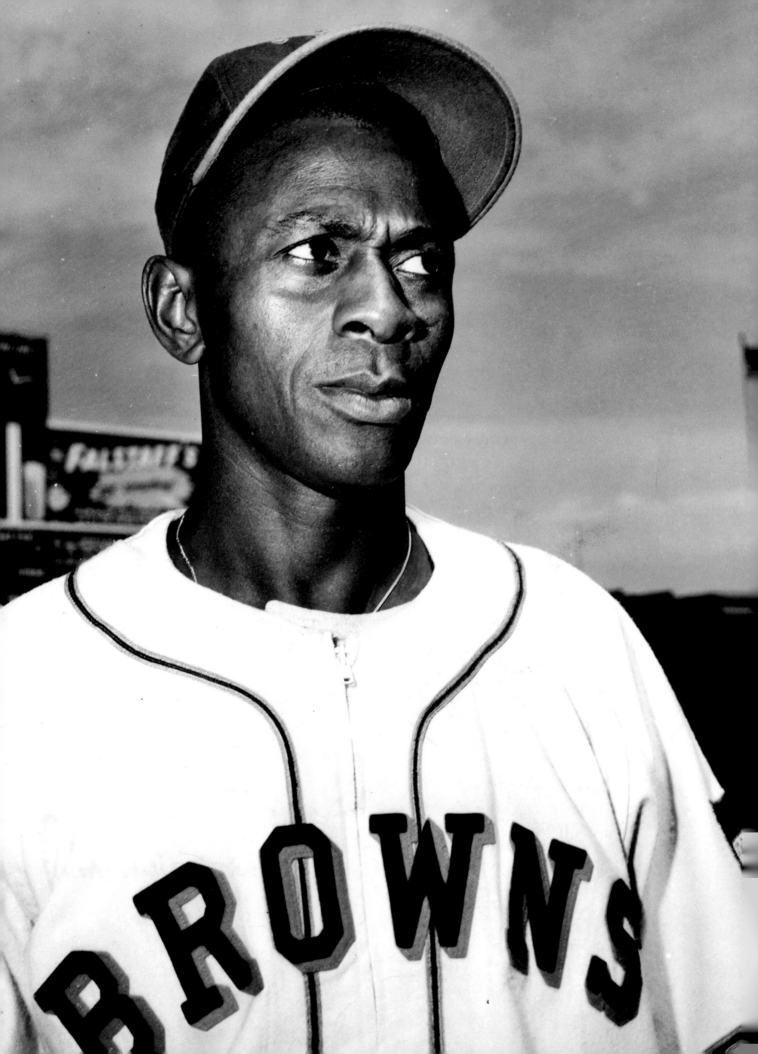

LEROY "SATCHEL" PAIGE

Inducted in 1971 by Special Committee on the Negro Leagues
Years with the Browns 1908–1910

1948–1949, 1951–1953, 1965	W	L	W-L%	ERA	G	GS	CG	SHO	SV	IP
6 Seasons	28	31	.475	3.29	179	26	7	4	32	476.0

At a time when the absurd became the norm and the bizarre the ordinary, one name stood out as one who actually backed up those incredible stories from the Negro Baseball Leagues.

Satchel Paige.

Of all the stories that came along with such colorful players as "Cool Papa" Bell, Judy Johnson, Buck Leonard, Josh Gibson, and even "Mule" Suttles and "Turkey" Stearnes, the fireballing pitcher may have been the most legendary folk hero in an era that didn't allow black players to play in the major leagues.

But Satchel's talents finally did bring him to the majors when he became the oldest rookie ever to play in the league when, at the ripe old age of forty-two, he was signed by the Cleveland Indians. Although he possessed a wild, windmill delivery, he had excellent control. His distinctive pitches included the "two-hump blooper," a moving changeup; "Little Tom," a medium fastball; "Long Tom," his hard fastball (also called his "bee ball"); and the controversial "hesitation pitch," for which he momentarily stopped his delivery halfway through.

He is perhaps best known for his maxim: "Don't look back. Something might be gaining on you."

Born Leroy Robert Paige in Mobile, Alabama, the slender 6′3½″ Paige was the seventh of eleven children (some reports say sixth of twelve) to a gardener and washerwoman. His nickname comes from his youth, when he had a job lugging suitcases at a train depot. He rigged a pole and some rope to carry three or four bags at once, prompting others to call him Satchel.

He joined his first organized team at the age of ten and soon developed a reputation as one of Mobile's best schoolboy players. But he was also known as a troublemaker, frequently playing hooky and getting into gang fights. At age twelve he was sent to the Industrial School for Negro Children after a shoplifting incident. Paige later reportedly said that those five and a half years at the reform institution "made a man out of me . . . and gave me a chance to polish up my baseball game. You might say I traded five years of freedom to learn how to pitch."

LEROY ROBERT PAIGE
"SATCHEL"
NEGRO LEAGUES   1926·1947
CLEVELAND A.L.   1948·1949
ST. LOUIS A.L.   1951·1953
KANSAS CITY A.L.   1965
PAIGE WAS ONE OF THE GREATEST STARS
TO PLAY IN THE NEGRO BASEBALL LEAGUES.
THRILLED MILLIONS OF PEOPLE AND WON
HUNDREDS OF GAMES. STRUCK OUT 21 MAJOR
LEAGUERS IN AN EXHIBITION GAME. HELPED
PITCH CLEVELAND INDIANS TO THE 1948
PENNANT IN HIS FIRST BIG LEAGUE YEAR
AT AGE 42. HIS PITCHING WAS A LEGEND
AMONG MAJOR LEAGUE HITTERS.

And polish he did.

In 1924, at the age of eighteen, he brought his array of pitches to the semipro Mobile Tigers and even though records weren't kept in those days, he said he won 30 games while losing only one. Then his travels began.

Over the next two decades he pitched wherever he could—for the Birmingham Black Barons, Nashville Elite Giants, Cleveland Cubs, Pittsburgh Crawfords, and nine seasons for the Kansas City Monarchs. He also barnstormed, often opposing the best major league players and even went to Mexico, Venezuela, and the Dominican Republic, drawing huge crowds everywhere.

Pitching for the Crawfords from 1932 to 1937, Paige, according to one source, went 23-7 in 1932, then won 31 of 35 decisions in 1933, including 21 straight wins and 62 consecutive scoreless innings. Paige himself claimed to have won 104 of 105 games in 1934.

Although he compiled impressive Negro League records, his exhibition performances became legendary. He often called in his outfielders before an inning and struck out the side. In 1934 he toured with Dizzy Dean and won four of the six games they pitched against each other. The following year, Joe DiMaggio called Paige "the best I've ever faced and the fastest."

Dean reportedly added: "My fastball looks like a change of pace alongside that pistol bullet old Satch shoots up to the plate. If Satch and I were pitching on the same team, we'd clinch the pennant by the Fourth of July and go fishing until World Series time."

With the Monarchs for most of the 1940s, Paige sparked the Kansas City squad in its annual battle with the Homestead Grays. And during the Negro League World Series in 1942, Paige won three of the four victories over the Grays.

In 1947 the major league color barrier was cracked when Brooklyn signed Jackie Robinson. Cleveland owner Bill Veeck signed Larry Doby as the first black American League player. And then on July 7, 1948, Paige's forty-second birthday, the Indians signed him as the first black pitcher in the AL.

Veeck reportedly said of the controversial signing: "If Satch were white, of course he would have been in the majors 25 years earlier."

The signing paid immediate dividends. Paige went 6-1 with a 2.48 ERA the rest of the way, helping the Indians to the World Series championship. He also brought out the crowds. More than 200,000 came to see his first three starts, including a Cleveland single-game record of 78,382.

When Veeck sold the Indians after the '49 season, Paige was released. But Veeck resurfaced as the Browns' owner in '51, again signing Satchel. Paige pitched in St. Louis for three seasons, going 12-10 in '52 with 10 saves and a league-high eight relief victories. On September 25, 1965, he became the oldest to pitch in the major leagues. Ever the showman, the fifty-nine-year-old Paige sat in a rocking chair in the bullpen while a nurse rubbed liniment on his arm.

When he was released by St. Louis, he continued his barnstorming ways before finishing his major league career with a three-inning stint for the Kansas City A's in September 1965. He was given a job as a pitching coach by Atlanta in 1968–1969, to help him gain his pension.

When Paige was asked about his longevity in baseball, he reportedly commented: "Age is a case of mind over matter. If you don't mind, it don't matter."

In 1971 he became the first of the Negro League stars to be elected to the Hall of Fame by the Committee on Negro Baseball Leagues.

1901–1917	W	L	W-L%	ERA	G	GS	CG	SHO	SV	IP
13 Seasons	326	194	.627	2.35	623	529	410	69	23	4495.2

Eddie Plank, nicknamed Gettysburg Eddie after his hometown, lived early and lived short, but managed to create a Hall of Fame career as a left-handed pitcher. Born in 1875, he went straight from Gettysburg College to the major leagues. Plank played for the Philadelphia Athletics for thirteen seasons, the St. Louis Terriers for one season, and finished with the St. Louis Browns.

Most would say they never heard of the man, but his credentials need no explanation. In 1941 Hall of Famer Eddie Collins said of Plank, "He wasn't the fastest pitcher, not the trickiest, and not the possessor of the best stuff, but he was the greatest pitcher in baseball!"

Legendary Ty Cobb agreed. He put Plank on his all-time pitching staff for his "great pure stuff and consistent control."

His days in St. Louis were brief. In 1915 he pitched in 34 games, winning 16 and losing 15 with a solid earned run average of 2.33. His final season he went 5-6 in just 14 games with a 1.79 ERA.

He made his name with legendary owner-manager Connie Mack of the Athletics. He won 20 games for the first time in 1902, his second season, helping the A's win the American League pennant. He posted an even better campaign with 23 wins in 1903, and made his first World Series in 1905, losing to the champion New York Giants.

The A's were perennial contenders in those days. They went to the series in 1910 but Plank was hurt, and again in '11 where he won Game 2 and the A's won the World Series. In 1913 the A's and

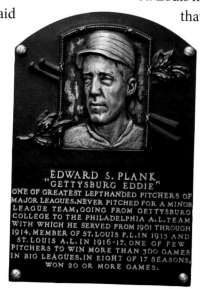

EDWARD S. PLANK
"GETTYSBURG EDDIE"
ONE OF GREATEST LEFTHANDED PITCHERS OF MAJOR LEAGUES. NEVER PITCHED FOR A MINOR LEAGUE TEAM, GOING FROM GETTYSBURG COLLEGE TO THE PHILADELPHIA A.L. TEAM WITH WHICH HE SERVED FROM 1901 THROUGH 1914. MEMBER OF ST. LOUIS F.L. IN 1915 AND ST. LOUIS A.L. IN 1916-17. ONE OF FEW PITCHERS TO WIN MORE THAN 300 GAMES IN BIG LEAGUES. IN EIGHT OF 17 SEASONS, WON 20 OR MORE GAMES.

Giants faced off again for the title, and Plank twice took on the great Christy Mathewson, winning Game 5 and losing Game 2, with his A's crowned as world champions.

Plank was a true superstar. He won 20 games in a season seven times and pitched six complete games in six tries in World Series competition, plus some relief appearances. His record was just 2-5, but not his fault with an ERA of 1.32!

St. Louis had a renegade Federal League team that grabbed Plank in 1914 when the A's were rumored to be trading him. His 21 wins with the Terriers were admitted to his major league records, giving him seven 20-win seasons.

Finally with the Browns, Plank had good intentions, wanting to play well for St. Louis. But arm problems that first appeared in 1910 plagued him, and he had trouble accepting that his baseball career was ending.

Gettysburg Eddie did rev it up one more time for the Browns. On August 6, 1917, he threw 11 brilliant innings, losing a heartbreaker 1-0 to Washington Senators Hall of Fame hurler Walter Johnson.

Plank's lifetime totals are remarkable. He was the first left-hander in history to win 200 games and then 300 games, finishing with 326 victories (eleventh all-time). He struck out 2,226, and holds the record for shutouts by a pitcher with 69!

Plank has many things named after him in Pennsylvania. He was inducted into the Baseball Hall of Fame posthumously in 1946. He died of a stroke at age fifty.

Inducted in 2006 • Years with the Cardinals 1981–1984

1976–1988	W	L	W-L%	ERA	G	GS	CG	SHO	SV	IP
12 Seasons	68	71	.489	2.83	661	0	0	0	300	1042

There are other rags to riches stories in the hallowed hallways of the Baseball Hall of Fame, and we're not talking about money. But the story of Bruce Sutter is amazing when you consider the odds of him turning a near-dead career with an injured arm into a Hall of Fame ending, all due to the development of one pitch.

The injury came right away. Signed by the Chicago Cubs in 1971 for five hundred dollars, he went to the Bradenton Cubs of the Gulf Coast League. After pitching in just two games, he was diagnosed with an elbow injury and was done for the 1972 season. Following an operation on the pinched nerve, he came to training camp in 1973, but—poof—no more fastball. Bruce paid for the surgery himself. "I didn't think an injured pitcher would get any chance at all, and I was afraid they would release me if they knew I was hurt," Sutter admitted. "I chose not to tell them because why would they pay for an untried pitcher and someone would say 'there goes another sore-armed pitcher.'"

Way down in Class A ball in Quincy, Illinois,

HOWARD BRUCE SUTTER
CHICAGO, N.L., 1976-1980
ST. LOUIS, N.L., 1981-1984
ATLANTA, N.L., 1985-1988

A DOMINANT CLOSER WHO REVOLUTIONIZED THE SPLIT-FINGERED FASTBALL, WHICH CONFOUNDED BATTERS. EARNED 300 SAVES AND POSTED A 2.83 ERA WHILE OFTEN PITCHING TWO OR MORE INNINGS. A SIX-TIME ALL-STAR SELECTION, RANKED AMONG THE TOP TEN IN NATIONAL LEAGUE MVP AND CY YOUNG VOTING FIVE TIMES EACH AND LED THE LEAGUE IN SAVES FIVE TIMES. WON 1979 N.L. CY YOUNG, POSTING 37 SAVES WHILE STRIKING OUT 110, ALLOWING 67 HITS IN 101.1 INNINGS. SAVED TWO GAMES AND RECORDED THE FINAL SIX OUTS FOR THE 1982 WORLD SERIES CHAMPION CARDINALS.

pitching instructor Fred Martin introduced the split-fingered fastball to Bruce in 1973. The pitch was not totally original, being a relative of the forkball, but with Sutter's long fingers, he could force it to spin forward and then dive downward as it reached home plate. His thumb would push the ball out from between his widespread fingers. Sutter still had just enough speed so the hitters couldn't tell whether it was a fastball or splitter.

Sutter's science was simple. He could change speeds with the pitch by simply changing the position of his arm in the delivery. He didn't change the speed of his arm, but when some of the balls would dive and bounce in front of the plate, it was more than a little unnerving to the batter.

After five years perfecting the pitch, Sutter made it to the majors as the Cubs' closer. In 1979 he had a banner year, with an NL-record-tying 37 saves and a 2.22 ERA. He became only the third relief pitcher in baseball history to win the Cy Young Award.

With Lee Smith waiting in the wings and

Sutter's large salary, the Cubs unloaded their star after the 1980 season. Cardinals manager Whitey Herzog stepped up in his new general manager's role, offering the Cubs the services of promising first baseman Leon Durham, St. Louis fan favorite Ken Reitz, and a minor leaguer named Ty Waller. Cardinal fans knew the game was over and a win would be recorded if Bruce Sutter came into the contest, whether it be in the eighth and ninth, as he would do often, or just in the ninth.

His Hall of Fame credentials were solidified after the 1982 championship, when he pumped his fist in celebration after saving Game 7 of the World Series, a sight that is well remembered in the Gateway City. Sutter, however, wasn't done. In 1984 he notched an NL-record 45 saves, with 122 innings (also a career high), five wins, and a nearly unhittable 1.54 ERA.

When Sutter was going into the hall, Herzog said in appreciation, "He was the most important guy on our team when we won. The way the game is played today, you are trying to cut the other team down to twenty-one outs to beat you. When you do that and you have Bruce Sutter ready to come in, you have a great chance to win."

He never started a game, becoming the first pitcher in history to enter the Hall of Fame exclusively as a reliever.

Pitching two innings to close a ball game was nothing for Sutter. Sometimes he'd even go more. From 1977 to 1984, he averaged more than 100 innings a season from the bullpen, and opposing bat-

Hall of Famers Ozzie Smith (left) and Lou Brock (right) celebrate Bruce Sutter's election to the hall at a Cooperstown party hosted by the Cardinals in 2006.

ters hit just .224. He won the NL's Rolaids Relief Award and the *Sporting News*'s Fireman of the Year Award four times, from 1979 to 1982. He led in saves three times as a Cardinal. Five times in his brilliant career he was a top-ten vote-getter for NL MVP.

Then, stunningly, the Cardinals lost their ace reliever. He accepted a six-year, $10 million free agent contract with the Atlanta Braves, but it didn't work out from the time he arrived. A pop in his shoulder came in spring training and he was never again the pitcher who stalked batters around the league. Still, at age thirty-five he had achieved twelve big league seasons in which he ran up 300 saves, third all-time, and was first in the NL to reach both 200 and 300 saves. His 127 saves as a Cardinal were the benchmark at the time.

"Bruuuu-ce," as the Cardinal fans would cry out each time their game-winning stopper appeared, is a member of the St. Louis Sports Hall of Fame and was inducted into the Baseball Hall of Fame in Cooperstown in 2006. He never started a game, becoming the first pitcher in history to enter the Hall of Fame exclusively as a reliever.

DAZZY VANCE

Inducted in 1955 • Years with the Cardinals 1933–1934

1915, 1918, 1922–1935	W	L	W-L%	ERA	G	GS	CG	SHO	SV	IP
16 Seasons	197	140	.585	3.24	442	349	216	29	11	2966.2

Charles Arthur "Dazzy" Vance, a nifty right-hander, had a brilliant career and earned Hall of Fame status long before coming to St. Louis. For the Cardinals he was mostly an insurance policy for a solid pitching staff in 1934. Vance didn't reach the major leagues permanently until he was thirty-one years old, in 1922, yet he still managed to win 197 games against 140 losses while compiling a 3.24 earned run average for five teams.

The author of a no-hit game while pitching for Brooklyn in 1925, Vance debuted with the Pittsburgh Pirates in 1915. He moved on to the New York Yankees, who made the mistake of letting him go in 1922 to the Brooklyn NL team, then called the Robins, with only eleven big league appearances under his belt. He would earn his Hall of Fame stripes in Brooklyn. He moved to the Cardinals, then to the Cincinnati Reds the next season, before coming back to the Cardinals to enjoy their 1934 championship. He retired after pitching for the Brooklyn Dodgers in 1935.

Despite the late start in the big leagues, the 6'2", 200-pounder had a hard fastball, which he threw with an imposing high leg kick. A wicked overhand curveball was even more impressive. In his first season with Brooklyn, Dazzy recorded a solid 18–12 record with a 3.70 ERA and 134 strikeouts in 245 innings. An 18–15 year followed, and then success really kicked in.

The year 1924 was his landmark MVP season. He went 28–6, had an ERA of 2.16, and struck out 262 hitters, leading the league in those three categories. He also pitched 30 complete games. In the second inning of a September 24 game against the Chicago Cubs, Vance struck out the side on nine pitches. He kept it going throughout the 1920s, leading the league in strikeouts from 1922 to 1928.

Vance started eleven games for the Cardinals in 1933 and went a respectable 6–2, completing eight of those games and appearing in a total of twenty-eight contests. In 1934 he saw action in nineteen games for the Cardinals, going 1–1.

The history books say his biggest contribution to the Cardinals in 1934 was his personality. He was a character, as his name may imply, and it seems appropriate that a raucous group called the Gashouse Gang would have a pair of pitchers named Dazzy and Dizzy! Dazzy's one appearance in the 1934 World Series was a relief job in the fourth game; he struck out three in an inning and a third.

Vance garnered his nickname as a boy in Nebraska. He was just eleven years old when he mimicked a cowboy who would say, "Ain't that a daisy" whenever he saw a horse, gun, or dog he liked. Except it sounded like "dazzy" when Vance said it. Dazzy Vance was inducted into the Baseball Hall of Fame in 1955.

RUBE WADDELL

Inducted in 1946 • Years with the Browns 1908–1910

1897, 1899–1910	W	L	W-L%	ERA	G	GS	CG	SHO	SV	IP
13 Seasons	193	143	.574	2.16	407	340	261	50	5	2961.1

Rube Waddell's baseball and personal life can only be described in one word—bizarre.

Even though many regard him as one of the finest left-handed pitchers in the history of the major leagues, the hulking hurler may also have been the consummate overgrown kid with his childish antics continually getting in the way of his career. His eccentric and colorful behavior and zany sprees made him one of baseball's true legends. But it was his great fastball and curve with pinpoint control that put him on a path to the Baseball Hall of Fame.

Some even said Waddell's exploits may have saved a floundering American League.

But first things first. George Edward "Rube" Waddell was born October 13, 1876. His father worked in the Pennsylvania oil fields for a division of Standard Oil. In fact, the nickname Rube was a faux pas, as fellow ballplayers thought he was a hayseed, brought up on a farm.

As he grew, Ed or Eddie, as his family called him, received a reputation as an excellent ballplayer while competing on semipro teams. That reputation earned him a tryout with

GEORGE EDWARD WADDELL
"RUBE"
COLORFUL LEFTHANDED PITCHER WHO WAS IN BOTH LEAGUES, BUT WHO GAINED FAME AS A MEMBER OF THE PHILADELPHIA A.L. TEAM. WON MORE THAN 20 GAMES IN FIRST FOUR SEASONS WITH THAT CLUB AND COMPILED MORE THAN 200 VICTORIES DURING MAJOR LEAGUE CAREER. WAS NOTED FOR HIS STRIKEOUT ACHIEVEMENTS.

Pittsburgh. But his unconventional mannerisms and short attention span (what many now call attention deficit disorder) during a breakfast meeting with manager Patsy Donovan quickly earned Waddell his release from the Pirates before he threw a single pitch.

However, the Louisville Colonels, then in the National League, liked his athleticism and signed him. He made his major league debut in 1897, but was sent to the minors for more "seasoning." In 1899 he gained success, going 26–8 with Columbus and Grand Rapids of the Western League. He rejoined Louisville the final month of the season and won seven of his nine decisions.

According to one report, the Louisville franchise was contracted from the National League in 1900, and the Colonels' owner purchased a half-interest in the Pirates. He arranged for the "trade" of ten of his players, including Waddell, to Pittsburgh.

Waddell went 8–13 that season, but he led NL pitchers in ERA (2.37) and was second in strikeouts (130), while missing nearly two months of the season. His irresponsible ways (missing starts to go fishing, playing marbles with neighborhood kids, or going AWOL for no apparent reason) didn't sit well with his Pittsburgh manager, Fred Clarke, and Waddell was suspended for the rest of the season.

It was while on suspension and playing for semi-pro teams that he caught Connie Mack's eye. Mack, who was managing Milwaukee of the American League, needed pitching. He struck a deal with Pittsburgh that he could sign Waddell, under the proviso that the Pirates could have him back if they needed pitching. Waddell thrived in Milwaukee, winning 10 games, before Pittsburgh wanted him back. Although the Waddell-Clarke relationship lasted through 1900, Rube was sold to the Chicago Orphans the following season. Waddell, however, left the Orphans midseason to go barnstorming with semi-pro teams again.

Mack never gave up trying to get Waddell to play for his team. In 1902 Mack, now managing the Philadelphia Athletics, finally induced Waddell to play for him again midway through the season. At age twenty-five, all the left-hander did was post a 24–7 mark, leading the league with 210 strikeouts, 50 more than Cy Young, who pitched 108⅓ more innings. Waddell's efforts also brought the Athletics their first pennant.

But Waddell continued to miss starts to go on his adventures and that behavior tested even the mild-mannered Mack, who normally had the patience to handle his southpaw hurler.

Some reports say Rube also had a fascination with fires. He often went to assist firefighters—from a bucket brigade in Pewaukee, Wisconsin, to large metropolitan departments in Philadelphia, Cleveland, Detroit, and Washington.

If Mack didn't have patience, Waddell probably wouldn't have lasted six seasons in Philadelphia—or on any major league roster for that matter. Waddell won 130 games in those six seasons with Mack and Philly. He led the AL in strikeouts six consecutive years and in 1904 he struck out 349, which remains the best strikeout total for an AL left-hander. His career ERA of 2.16 is still the best by any left-hander

in major league history.

In 1905 he led the AL with a 1.48 ERA, 27 victories, and 287 strikeouts—pitching's Triple Crown. However, Waddell missed most of the final month of the season when he injured his shoulder in a fall during a friendly argument over a straw hat with a teammate. Mack felt Waddell was never the same after that.

Meanwhile, Rube's pitching ability and showmanship added to his legend and, as his win totals grew, so too did the fans who came to watch him. Those huge crowds helped the financially ailing American League.

"Rube's activity with Connie Mack's band virtually saved the American League from bankruptcy," wrote the *Pittsburgh Press* shortly after Waddell's death in 1914. The *Milwaukee Sentinel* added: "Let it be said now that Waddell saved the American League from the rocks of bankruptcy."

Waddell's antics and drinking problems finally spelled the end of the Waddell-Mack relationship. In 1908 Mack sold the southpaw to St. Louis, where he would spend his final three seasons in the majors. Waddell won 19 games his first year with the Browns, still drawing huge crowds. The Browns' home attendance reportedly rose forty-eight percent that first year, while Philadelphia's crowds dipped thirty percent.

"He paid for himself in three games after he was bought," wrote *St. Louis Post-Dispatch* columnist John L. Wray. "He had added many thousands to the exchecquer [sic] since that time—paid admissions that would never have arrived at the gate but for the fact that Rube was scheduled to work."

However, Rube appeared in only ten games his third season in St. Louis, all but two in relief, and the Browns released him in August.

Waddell contracted pneumonia and then tuberculosis and died April 1, 1914.

After his death, Mack said: "He was the greatest pitcher in the game, and although widely known for his eccentricities, was more sinned against than sinner. He may have failed us at times but to him, I and the other owners of the Athletics ball club, owe much."

HOYT WILHELM

Inducted in 1985 • Year with the Cardinals 1957

1952–1972	W	L	W-L%	ERA	G	GS	CG	SHO	SV	IP
21 Seasons	143	122	.540	2.52	1070	52	20	5	227	2254.1

Call it another one of those "quick claims" to include one of the game's greatest knuckleball pitchers of all time on the list of Cardinals in the Hall of Fame. As much as Cardinals fans would have wanted the great Old Sarge in their bullpen for many seasons, he actually spent just the 1957 campaign wearing the birds on the bat.

There was good reason to grab the then thirty-three-year-old right-hander from the New York Giants for backup first baseman Whitey Lockman. The Cardinals had a good ball club and were in the hunt until very late in the season. They finished in second place, eight games behind the pennant-winning Milwaukee Braves. Unfortunately, it wasn't a banner year for Wilhelm, who went 1–4 with an ERA of 4.25 in 55 innings.

Wilhelm was largely responsible for creating the role of the relief pitcher when he signed on with the New York Giants in 1952 at the not-so-tender age of twenty-nine. Relievers had been used sparingly in baseball in the late 1940s, but Wilhelm set the new standard. He had a brilliant 15–3 record in 1952, pitching in 71 games, getting 11 saves in 159.1 innings. He also struck out 108 batters and had an ERA of 2.43, again, all in relief.

He was off and running in a career that would span twenty seasons, taking him to age forty-nine. He was an all-star in 1953, 1959, 1961, 1962, and 1970. His best season was 1965 while

JAMES HOYT WILHELM
NEW YORK N.L., 1952-1956   ST. LOUIS N.L., 1957
CLEVELAND A.L., 1957-1958   BALTIMORE A.L., 1958-1962
CHICAGO A.L., 1963-1968   CALIFORNIA A.L., 1969
ATLANTA N.L., 1969-1970, 1971   CHICAGO N.L., 1970
LOS ANGELES N.L., 1971-1972
BASEBALL'S PREMIER RELIEF PITCHER. USED KNUCKLE
BALL TO WIN 143 GAMES (A RECORD 124 IN RELIEF)
AND AMASSED 227 SAVES OVER 21-YEAR CAREER.
NO-HIT YANKEES ON SEPT. 20, 1958 IN INFREQUENT
START FOR ORIOLES. PITCHED IN RECORD 1070
GAMES WITH LIFETIME ERA OF 2.52.

playing with the Chicago White Sox. There, Hoyt won 7 games, saved 20, pitched 144 innings in 66 relief appearances, struck out 106 hitters, and gave up just 88 hits with 32 walks. Best of all his ERA was 1.81.

Wilhelm was truly a pacesetter, pitching in baseball's golden era against the great ones. Willie Mays, Stan Musial, Henry Aaron, Mickey Mantle, Ted Williams, Frank Robinson, Pete Rose, Reggie Jackson, and Steve Garvey were among those who withered in the face of his floating knuckler. He saw them all because, despite his consistency, he played with nine different teams and in both leagues.

Wilhelm garnered the occasional start during his long career. His most memorable start came on September 20, 1958, when he sailed through the ever-threatening lineup of the soon-to-be world champion New York Yankees. The result was his only no-hit game. The Yanks were loaded with stars like Mantle, Hank Bauer, and Yogi Berra. Forty-five years would pass before the Yanks were no-hit again in 2003.

Hoyt Wilhelm was the top reliever of his era. He had this to say about his game: "I don't even try to fool anybody. I just throw the knuckleball 85 to 90 percent of the time. You don't need variations, because the damn ball jumps around so crazily. It's like having a hundred pitches." He took his knuckleball into the Baseball Hall of Fame in 1985, breaking the ice for relief pitchers.

WILLIS, ST. LOUIS NAT'L

WILLIS, ST. LOUIS NAT'L

VIC WILLIS

Inducted in 1995 • Year with the Cardinals 1910

1898–1910	W	L	W-L%	ERA	G	GS	CG	SHO	SV	IP
13 Seasons	249	205	.548	2.63	513	471	388	50	11	3996

With a smooth, graceful delivery from his tall frame, right-hander Vic Willis must have mirrored Hall of Fame lefty Steve Carlton in his day. The Cardinals saw Willis only briefly and not at his best. When he arrived in St. Louis for the 1910 season, he was beginning to have arm trouble. His nine wins for the Cardinals were a pittance compared to the 249 total wins he amassed primarily with Boston and Pittsburgh. The Birds went 63–90 for a seventh-place spot in the league, and it was their seventh straight season losing 90 or more games. It was Willis's final season in baseball.

Willis won 20 games eleven times. Oddly, on three occasions, he reached the mark in the loss column, including a record 25 losses in 1904. Two years earlier, he finished with a record of 27–20.

Everyone knows the Georgia Peach—the immortal Ty Cobb—but Willis was dubbed the Delaware Peach, a name given to him because of his days at the University of Delaware. Born in 1876, he jumped to the big leagues at age twenty-two as a tall, intimidating right-hander with a vicious curveball. Willis roared out of the gate in his rookie season, posting a 25–13 record with a 2.84 ERA, shouldering a lot of the responsibility for Boston's six-game edge in winning the NL pennant. He hurled 311 innings and completed 29 games in

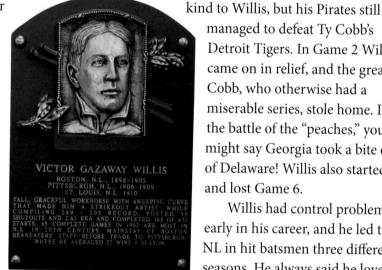

41 starts. In his career, he notched an astonishing 388 complete games, and that includes 139 complete-game losses.

For all those innings and all those victories, a championship season was a long time coming for Willis. He didn't sip the champagne until he was traded to Pittsburgh. In 1909 Honus Wagner led the Pirates to a championship, and Willis won 22 of the team's 110 victories that season.

Unfortunately, the World Series wasn't kind to Willis, but his Pirates still managed to defeat Ty Cobb's Detroit Tigers. In Game 2 Willis came on in relief, and the great Cobb, who otherwise had a miserable series, stole home. In the battle of the "peaches," you might say Georgia took a bite out of Delaware! Willis also started and lost Game 6.

Willis had control problems early in his career, and he led the NL in hit batsmen three different seasons. He always said he loved to bat as well, but his hitting stats weren't great. He had a .166 career batting mark, the second worst in baseball history for players with 1,400 at-bats or more.

In fairness, by the time he came to the Cardinals, Willis was having arm problems, no doubt due to all those innings and complete games. The Veterans Committee saw fit to induct him into the Baseball Hall of Fame forty-eight years after his death, in 1995.

CY YOUNG

Inducted in 1937 • Years with the Cardinals 1899–1900

1890–1911	W	L	W-L%	ERA	G	GS	CG	SHO	SV	IP
22 Seasons	511	316	.618	2.63	906	815	749	76	17	7354.2

Denton True "Cy" Young's name is synonymous with pitching excellence. In 1956 Major League Baseball named an award in honor of his pitching accomplishments, which include amassing more victories and more innings pitched than any pitcher in the history of the game. Cy Young pitched for twenty-two years around the turn of the twentieth century, including two seasons with the St. Louis National League entry. His 511 victories still stand as a barometer of pitching excellence. And if 511 victories are hard to fathom, imagine that he also pitched an all-time high of 7,354.2 innings. Neither of those records is likely to ever be broken.

Although record keeping back in the late 1800s and early 1900s is often in dispute (his victory total has been reported anywhere from 509 to 511), it is known that he pitched the first perfect game in the modern era. Big in his day at 6'2", 210 pounds, Young was a fireballing right-hander who earned the nickname The Cyclone. It seems the nickname originated when Young threw a fastball against a wooden fence, knocking out several boards. Someone mentioned that it looked like a cyclone had torn the boards loose.

Young later attributed his stamina to working on the Ohio farm where he was raised. That hard work reportedly kept him away from school a good deal of the time, and he never went past the sixth grade. But at the age of twenty-three, realizing his natural gift as a ballplayer, he embarked on a pitching career. Young actually started as a third baseman for his amateur team but quickly turned to pitching. In his first major league season with Cleveland, then known as the Spiders, Young posted a 9–7 record—the only pitcher on the team with a winning mark. However, over the next nineteen years he averaged almost 27 victories a season. He won 20 or more games in sixteen seasons, including five when he captured 30 or more victories. His best season came in 1892 when he won 36 games, 9 by shutouts, and had a 1.93 earned run average—all league highs. That season, he also pitched a whopping 453 innings.

Following the 1893 season, the mound was moved back from 55 feet, 6 inches, to the present-day 60 feet, 6 inches. The change, however,

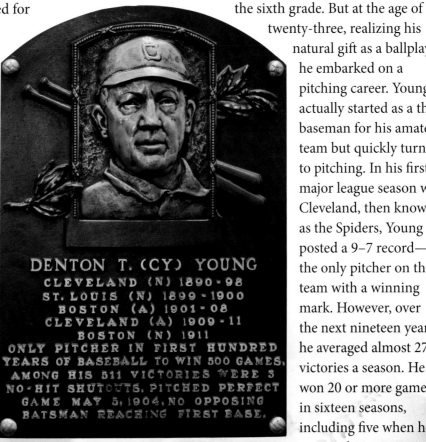

DENTON T. (CY) YOUNG
CLEVELAND (N) 1890-98
ST. LOUIS (N) 1899-1900
BOSTON (A) 1901-08
CLEVELAND (A) 1909-11
BOSTON (N) 1911
ONLY PITCHER IN FIRST HUNDRED
YEARS OF BASEBALL TO WIN 500 GAMES,
AMONG HIS 511 VICTORIES WERE 3
NO-HIT SHUTOUTS. PITCHED PERFECT
GAME MAY 5, 1904, NO OPPOSING
BATSMAN REACHING FIRST BASE.

didn't affect Young's exploits as it did some other pitchers of the day. Instead, Cy seemed to flourish. He won 34 games the following season, and two years later won 35.

Young's path to the Cardinals took a circuitous route before the 1899 season. It seems the Robison brothers, Frank and Stanley, who owned the Cleveland Spiders, purchased the St. Louis NL team (then known as the Browns). With attendance down in Cleveland, the brothers felt St. Louis might be a better market, and they moved many of their players, including Young, from the Spiders to the Browns, whose name they changed to the Perfectos for a season, and then the Cardinals.

Now thirty-two years old, Young posted a 26–16 record with St. Louis in 1899, during which he started 42 games and completed 40. The following year, however, Young went a mediocre 19–19, as the Cardinals had a poor season. The Robison brothers criticized Young for his effort that season, causing a rift between owner and player.

Young posted a 26–16 record with St. Louis in 1899, during which he started 42 games and completed 40.

The timing of the discord couldn't have been worse for the future of the Cardinals. The American League had just gained major league status and began a bidding war for the National League's top performers. Young signed a three-year contract with Boston for $3,500, and over the next three years, he led the AL with 33, 32, and 28 victories, debunking any notion that he was past his prime. That first season with Boston also was one of the best all-around years of Young's career. Besides his 33–10 record, he also had the league's lowest ERA (1.62) and led the league in

strikeouts. Young also led Boston to its first World Series championship, starting three games and pitching in a fourth.

The big right-hander still wasn't through. In 1904, during a game in which he faced Philadelphia ace and future Hall of Famer Rube Waddell, Young pitched the first perfect game since the mound was moved back to 60 feet, 6 inches. The 3–0 victory began a string of 45 consecutive scoreless innings for Young that included 24 straight no-hit frames.

Young was voted into the Baseball Hall of Fame in 1937. The Cy Young Award, originated in 1956 for the major league's best pitcher, has since been given to the most outstanding pitcher in each league.

The 1899 St. Louis Perfectos. Cy Young is at the far left of the front row.

CHAPTER 5
MANAGERS and OWNERS

Inducted in 1983 • Year with the Cardinals 1936

1954–1976	G	W	L	W-L%
23 Seasons	3658	2040	1613	.558

There is a popular saying among knowledgeable baseball aficionados that the best managers were only borderline players. This belief can certainly be attributed to Walter Alston, whose entire major league record consists of one at-bat—with the Cardinals in 1936. However, the easygoing Alston went on to post a managerial record of more than 2,000 wins, seven pennants, and four World Series, a record that led him to the Hall of Fame.

Alston was a first baseman with the Cardinals in the 1936 season. His only appearance came on September 27, as a substitute for future Hall of Famer Johnny Mize, who had been ejected from the game. Alston struck out. He then returned to the minor leagues where he toiled as a player before getting the opportunity to become a player-manager.

After earning his college degree in 1932 and teaching for a few years, Alston signed a minor league contract with the Cardinals in 1935. He tried almost every position during a thirteen-year minor league playing career (1935–1947).

In 1940, when it became apparent that he wasn't in the Cardinals' future plans as a player, Alston was given the opportunity to play and manage Portsmouth in the Mid-Atlantic League, where he guided the team to a sixth-place finish. After two more years, Alston was promoted to Rochester as a player only. He was released by St. Louis in 1944 but signed by former Cardinals

general manager and then-Brooklyn president Branch Rickey to play and manage in the Dodgers' minor league system. In 1946 Rickey chose Alston as one of two skippers to manage black players by placing Don Newcombe and Roy Campanella on his Nashua, New Hampshire, team. From 1948 to 1953, Walt managed at the Triple-A level. He led St. Paul to the American Association championship in 1949 and was immediately promoted to the Dodgers' top minor league job in Montreal. Alston spent four seasons with Montreal and managed many players who went on to help win pennants for the big league club.

WALTER EMMONS ALSTON

SOFT-SPOKEN, LOW-PROFILE ORGANIZATION MAN WHO MANAGED THE DODGERS FOR 23 YEARS, LEADING TEAM TO ITS ONLY WORLD CHAMPIONSHIP IN BROOKLYN IN 1955 AND TO PENNANT IN 1956 BEFORE TEAM MOVED TO WEST COAST. IN LOS ANGELES HIS CLUBS WON WORLD TITLES IN 1959, 1963 AND 1965 AND PENNANTS IN 1966 AND 1974; AND ONLY JOHN MCGRAW, WITH 10, TOPPED ALSTON'S SEVEN N.L. PENNANTS. TEAMS FINISHED IN FIRST DIVISION 18 TIMES, WINNING 2,040 GAMES.

Following the 1953 season, Brooklyn manager Charlie Dressen insisted on a multi-year contract. Owner Walter O'Malley balked at the demand, and to everyone's surprise he chose the little-known Alston to pilot the club. Walt led the Dodgers to a second-place finish in 1954, then won the pennant and Brooklyn's only World Series championship in 1955, defeating the Yankees in seven games. He followed that with another pennant in 1956, securing his position as Dodger field boss, and continued his ritual of extending his stay as manager on one-year contracts. Alston won seven pennants in his twenty-three years as Dodgers manager. He was named NL Manager of the Year six times and led NL All-Star teams to seven victories. The Veterans Committee elected him into the Hall of Fame in 1983.

1909–1912, 1915	G	W	L	W-L%
5 Seasons	775	328	432	.432

Roger Bresnahan, who played for and managed the St. Louis Cardinals for four seasons, was one of the top catchers in baseball in the first decade of the 1900s and was the player both John McGraw and Branch Rickey considered the finest catcher they ever saw. He was also a key member of the New York Giants club that won the 1905 World Series.

Bresnahan was nicknamed the Duke of Tralee because he told people he was born in Tralee, Ireland. In reality, he was born and died in Toledo, Ohio, and is the only Toledoan to be enshrined in the Hall of Fame. He was the first catcher elected to Cooperstown. In all, Bresnahan played six positions in the majors, mostly as a catcher, where he caught in 974 games. He played 281 games in the outfield, 42 at third base, 33 at first base, 9 as a right-handed hurler, and 8 at shortstop.

The Duke began his career playing for a team in Lima, Ohio, and was an eighteen-year-old pitcher for the 1897 Washington Senators, going 4–0 with a 3.95 ERA in six appearances. After playing a few seasons with the Toledo Mud

ROGER BRESNAHAN

BATTERY MATE OF CHRISTY MATHEWSON WITH THE NEW YORK GIANTS, HE WAS ONE OF THE GAME'S MOST NATURAL PLAYERS AND MIGHT HAVE STARRED AT ANY POSITION. THE "DUKE OF TRALEE" WAS ONE OF THE FEW MAJOR LEAGUE CATCHERS FAST ENOUGH TO BE USED AS A LEADOFF MAN.

Hens, he returned to the majors in 1900 with the Chicago Orphans, appearing in two games as a catcher. He spent the next season and a half with the Baltimore Orioles, splitting time between the outfield and behind the plate.

Midway through the 1902 campaign, Bresnahan, pitcher Joe McGinnity, and manager John McGraw jumped from the Orioles to the New York Giants of the National League, the club with which he would have his greatest seasons. The compact and pugnacious performer hit .350 and, although a catcher, stole 34 bases with the team in 1903. In the 1905 World Series, he caught a record four shutouts (three by Christy Mathewson and another by Joe McGinnity) while batting .313 at the leadoff position.

After spending eight seasons with the New York Giants, Bresnahan was traded after the 1908 season to the Cardinals, for whom he was also given the opportunity to manage. Although the Duke was on the decline, he got a sweetheart deal from the Cardinal ownership. The Cardinals had a mediocre team under Bresnahan's leadership and finished in the second division in each of his four years at the helm—seventh, seventh, fifth, and sixth. Actually, his 1911 team was in the pennant race for a good part of the season, but they fell back to fifth place, one game over the .500 mark. Meanwhile, because of his managerial duties, he saw only part-time duty on the field.

He was the first catcher elected to Cooperstown. In all, Bresnahan played six positions in the majors, mostly as a catcher, where he caught in 974 games.

After playing in only forty-eight games and hitting .333 in 1912, his final season with the Cardinals, he was released by the club after a confrontation with team owner Helene Hathaway Robison Britton, the first female owner in Major League Baseball. In fact, in 1911 Bresnahan led a group of investors who unsuccessfully tried to purchase the club from Britton. Bresnahan was

picked up by the Chicago Cubs, for whom he played and also managed until 1915, his final season as both a big league player and skipper.

However, protective gear was his most notable contribution to baseball. After being served a beanball in 1905, he experimented with a leather batting helmet. Although beanballs were common, the helmet took years to catch on. He followed this novelty by introducing catcher shin guards and improvements to the catcher's mask. The shin guards, although ridiculed at the outset, caught on quickly.

The Veterans Committee inducted him into the Baseball Hall of Fame in 1945.

BRESNAHAN (St. Louis Nationals)

BRESNAHAN
Catcher, St. Louis N. L.

BRESNAHAN, ST. LOUIS NAT'L

CARDINALS

Roger P. Bresnahan

OF THE
ST. LOUIS NATIONALS

ROGER BRESNAHAN

1973–1990	G	W	L	W-L%
18 Seasons	2409	1281	1125	.532

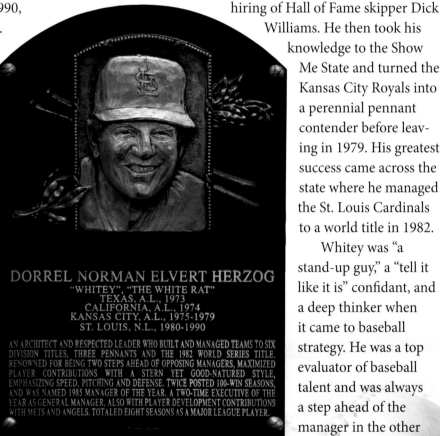

DORREL NORMAN ELVERT HERZOG
"WHITEY", "THE WHITE RAT"
TEXAS, A.L., 1973
CALIFORNIA, A.L., 1974
KANSAS CITY, A.L., 1975-1979
ST. LOUIS, N.L., 1980-1990

AN ARCHITECT AND RESPECTED LEADER WHO BUILT AND MANAGED TEAMS TO SIX
DIVISION TITLES, THREE PENNANTS AND THE 1982 WORLD SERIES TITLE.
RENOWNED FOR BEING TWO STEPS AHEAD OF OPPOSING MANAGERS, MAXIMIZED
PLAYER CONTRIBUTIONS WITH A STERN YET GOOD-NATURED STYLE,
EMPHASIZING SPEED, PITCHING AND DEFENSE. TWICE POSTED 100-WIN SEASONS,
AND WAS NAMED 1985 MANAGER OF THE YEAR. A TWO-TIME EXECUTIVE OF THE
YEAR AS GENERAL MANAGER, ALSO WITH PLAYER DEVELOPMENT CONTRIBUTIONS
WITH METS AND ANGELS. TOTALED EIGHT SEASONS AS A MAJOR LEAGUE PLAYER.

Baseball fans knew long before the baseball writers voted "yes" that Dorrell Norman Elvert "Whitey" Herzog belonged in the Hall of Fame. He revived baseball interests in two Missouri cities, Kansas City and St. Louis. In all, he won six division titles, three pennants, and one World Series between 1975 and 1990, managing thirteen seasons.

As a player from 1956 to 1963, he was a left-handed batter and roamed the outfield in Washington, Kansas City, Baltimore, and Detroit. Statistically, he batted .254 with 25 home runs, 172 runs batted in, and even stole 13 bases in 634 major league games. Whitey famously quipped, "Baseball has been good to me since I quit trying to play it."

However, as a manager, he rose to the top of his profession. He gives a lot of credit to the wisdom learned from his first manager and later close friend, Casey Stengel, the New York Yankees and Mets legend. Herzog learned from the ground up, as a scout, a third base coach, a director of player development, and finally as a manager and then general manager.

"Whitey," as he's affectionately known, was nicknamed by a sportscaster in McAlester, Oklahoma, named Bill Speith. Whitey had four managerial stops. He took on a disaster with the Texas Rangers in 1973—"the worst excuse for a ball club I ever saw"—then on to the California Angels in 1974 as an interim manager before their hiring of Hall of Fame skipper Dick Williams. He then took his knowledge to the Show Me State and turned the Kansas City Royals into a perennial pennant contender before leaving in 1979. His greatest success came across the state where he managed the St. Louis Cardinals to a world title in 1982.

Whitey was "a stand-up guy," a "tell it like it is" confidant, and a deep thinker when it came to baseball strategy. He was a top evaluator of baseball talent and was always a step ahead of the manager in the other dugout. The Kansas City and St. Louis teams didn't need a team captain with Herzog running the ship.

His Royals won American League Western Division titles in 1976, 1977, and 1978. Each time they fell short of the pennant because of the New York Yankees. He coached great players like Hall of Famer George Brett, Willie Wilson,

Amos Otis, Dennis Leonard, Brett Saberhagen, and catcher Darrell Porter. He took over for manager Jack McKeon during the 1975 season, with the team struggling. He reversed the team's direction and almost won that year, finishing 91–71, a mark of 41–25 under Herzog. In the postseason, frustration reigned as the Yankees had just enough to beat Kansas City. In each of the first two playoff series, the Royals went into the ninth inning tied or ahead only to lose the deciding Game 5. In 1978 the Royals were beaten three games to one by New York, and in 1979 the team slipped to 85 wins and no playoffs, leading to Herzog's dismissal.

Herzog's release was a blessing for the St. Louis Cardinals. Owner August A. Busch Jr. called Whitey in June to replace his struggling manager, Ken Boyer. By Labor Day, Herzog was in control of the team as manager and general manager, and he put Hall of Famer Red Schoendienst in charge on the field for the final month so he could concentrate on evaluating the club and making changes. Herzog dealt players like a deck of cards and totally rebuilt the sagging franchise. He sent favorites catcher Ted Simmons and third baseman Ken Reitz packing along with a string of others and ended up with Hall of Fame relief ace Bruce Sutter and his favorite catcher and a leader at Kansas City, Darrell Porter.

The Redbirds nearly won the division in 1981 but were edged out by a numbers game caused by a player walkout. The season was played in halves, and although the Cardinals would have won the Eastern Division using the whole season's record, they did not win either the first half or second half as separate entities, finishing second in both.

Four more acquisitions put the White Rat into a position to win. The Cardinals acquired outfielders Willie McGee from the Yankees system, Lonnie Smith from Cleveland, pitcher Joaquin Andujar from Houston, and the all-important Ozzie Smith at shortstop from San Diego. The surrounding cast included second baseman Tommy Herr, first baseman Keith Hernandez, and third baseman Ken Oberkfell. Silent George Hendrick served the purpose in right field and a bevy of pitchers including Bob Forsch and John Stuper made it work in 1982.

The Cardinals used what was called "Whitey Ball" to win the division with a record of 92–70, then got by the round he couldn't win at Kansas City, sweeping the Atlanta Braves to earn a World Series trip. They won a hard-fought seven-game series, with Herzog using the whole roster to his advantage. Darrell Porter was named the Most Valuable Player, and the last out belonged to Bruce Sutter.

After two down years, Herzog retooled for two more great seasons: 1985 and 1987. The 1985 Cardinals were dominant, going 101–61, winning by just three games over the New York Mets. Herzog won the Manager of the Year award while his center fielder, McGee, was voted NL MVP. In the playoffs, Herzog's nine defeated the National League opponents and faced his old Kansas City Royals as the heavy favorites in the World Series. The Cards rolled to a three games to two lead into Game 6 in Kansas City. A bad call in the bottom of the ninth inning with the Cardinals leading 1–0 led to two Royals runs and a win. The momentum carried over to Game 7, and Kansas City brought home the championship.

In 1987 the Cardinals regrouped again, playing

SEC. 368   ROW 13   SEAT 20

1982 WORLD SERIES
$18.00   GAME 6
TERRACE RESERVED
BUSCH MEMORIAL STADIUM

WORLD SERIES 1982

ST. LOUIS CARDINALS

VS.
AMERICAN LEAGUE CHAMPIONS

RAIN CHECK subject to the conditions set forth on back hereof.
DO NOT DETACH THIS COUPON
BOWIE K. KUHN,
Commissioner of Baseball
GAME 6

an exciting version of baseball based on speed, defense, and just enough power. A potent offense built a 9½-game lead in the standings by July 23, and while it shrunk to just 1½ on September 19, the ball club had a champagne party against Montreal on October 1. What would hurt in the playoffs was the loss of power hitter Jack Clark, who had 35 home runs and 106 RBIs in just 131 games; he severely

Herzog learned from the ground up, as a scout, a third base coach, a director of player development, and finally as a manager and then general manager.

sprained an ankle and tore ligaments in a slide on September 9.

The Redbirds pulled it together in the playoff round against the bad guys from San Francisco. Down three games to two and back at Busch Stadium for a crucial Game 6, a fabulous start by lefty John Tudor and a superlative finish by Whitey's famous "Bullpen by Committee" of Ken Dayley and Todd Worrell resulted in a 1–0 win. In Game 7 the Cardinals' Danny Cox shut out the Giants, 6–0, to advance to the World Series. The Minnesota Twins had home-field advantage, and the Cardinals lost the series, 4–3.

Herzog resigned during the 1990 season, ready for some quiet time fishing and getting away from a changing game. He got back in the game as a front office executive after a call from Los Angeles Angels owner Gene Autry. Autry was a man much like Mr. Busch in St. Louis, and he and Herzog

agreed on things. His respect for Whitey allowed the King of the Cowboys to let go of the reins of his ball club and let Herzog be in charge. He did it for two seasons, 1993–1994.

Whitey was proud of his many accomplishments, but one he relished was the entertainment he brought to St. Louis baseball fans. There was a twinkle in his eye when he said, "I'm really proud of the fact that we brought three million fans into the ballpark for the first time in Cardinals history in 1989 (3,080,980) and Mr. Busch got to see it."

His glistening resume complete—1,281 wins, 1,125 losses, and 38 years in the game—Whitey was voted by Cardinals fans as the best and most popular manager in the team's history. He was also Manager of the Year in 1982, and the Writers' Manager of the Year in 1985 for taking a team picked last in their division to the World Series. Finally, he was selected as the *Sports Illustrated* Manager of the Decade for the 1980s. He was elected to the Baseball Hall of Fame by the Veterans Committee in 2009.

MILLER HUGGINS

Inducted in 1964 • Years with the Cardinals 1910-1917

1913–1929	G	W	L	W-L%
17 Seasons	2570	1413	1134	.555

It would have been interesting if Miller Huggins had gotten his wish and purchased the St. Louis Cardinals. Known as the Mighty Mite as a player because of his slight stature—a scrawny 5'6", 140 pounds—Huggins had a law degree from the University of Cincinnati, and he invested well in the stock market. His good fortune allowed him to pull together a syndicate intent on buying the St. Louis club after he had served as a player and manager for seven seasons.

Hug, as he was also called, began his major league career in 1904 with his hometown Cincinnati Reds but was traded to the Cardinals in 1910 and became the team's player-manager in 1913. In five seasons, Huggins guided St. Louis to two third-place finishes, the best the team had done since 1876. A second baseman, Huggins was fast and sure-handed in the field. He hit a career-best .304 in 1912, but his career average was a mere .265. However, he regularly posted an on-base percentage near .400, scored 100 or more runs three times, and consistently stole 30 or more bases.

MILLER JAMES HUGGINS
1904-1929
MANAGER OF ST. LOUIS CARDINALS
AND NEW YORK YANKEES.
LED YANKEES TO 6 PENNANTS
IN 1921, 1922, 1923, 1926, 1927 AND 1928 AND
3 WORLD SERIES VICTORIES 1923, 1927 AND 1928.
SECOND BASEMAN IN PLAYING DAYS
WITH REDS AND CARDINALS, 1904-1916.

In 1918 Cardinal owner Helene "Lady Bee" Britton—the first female owner in Major League Baseball—rebuffed her manager's bid to purchase the team in favor of another offer. Branch Rickey replaced Huggins, whose leadership skills did not go unnoticed. Huggins went on to manage the powerful New York Yankees dynasty of the 1920s. From 1918 until his death late in 1929, he led murderer's row to the franchise's first six pennants and three world championships.

Huggins inherited an almost uncontrollable bunch of carousers and bad actors when he took over the team, and he shaped the Yanks into a squad that became one of baseball's all-time best. Many say a five thousand dollar fine and a nine-day suspension of Babe Ruth turned the team around after an appalling slump in 1925. After nine days, Ruth apologized, paid his fine, and began playing again. With the backing of Jacob Ruppert, the Yanks' principal owner, Huggins established himself as boss, beginning the club's tradition of Yankee pride. The team took off under Huggins's guidance and handling.

Among the teams that won six pennants

and three World Series under Huggins was the 1927 squad, considered by many to be the greatest in history. Although Huggins and Babe Ruth had more than a few rows, Ruth once stated that he never respected any man in baseball more than Huggins.

Hug died of erysipelas, a rare skin infection, on September 25, 1929, only five days after stepping down as manager. On May 30, 1932, the Yankees dedicated a monument to Huggins and placed it in front of the flagpole in center field at Yankee Stadium, the first of many Yankee legends honored in Monument Park.

As a manager, Huggins amassed 1,413 wins with 1,134 losses, a .555 percentage. He was elected to the Baseball Hall of Fame in 1964.

Miller Huggins talks things over with New York third baseman Art Devlin, 1910.

CARDINALS

Miller J Huggins

OF THE
ST. LOUIS NATIONALS

Miller Huggins and New York manager
John McGraw have a discussion with
umpire Bill Brennan, 1913.

TONY LARUSSA

Inducted in 2014 • Years with the Cardinals 1996–2011

1979–2011	G	W	L	W-L%
33 Seasons	5093	2728	2365	.536

Tony LaRussa Jr. is the winningest manager in the illustrious history of the St. Louis Cardinals with 1,408 wins, surpassing Hall of Famers Red Schoendienst and Whitey Herzog. He was the Cardinals' skipper for sixteen seasons from 1996 to 2012.

Then there is the hardware he earned for St. Louis. His teams won eight division titles (1996, 2000, 2001, 2002, 2004, 2005, 2006, 2009), three National League pennants (2004, 2006, 2011), and two World Series (2006, 2011). Also impressive are his thirteen seasons above .500 in sixteen tries, and the two 100-win seasons—105 in 2004 and 100 in 2005. Only manager Billy Southworth has equaled that achievement.

There are many more stats backing up LaRussa's induction as a first ballot Hall of Famer. During the first decade of the twenty-first century, his teams won a National League–leading 913 games, and also led with 33 postseason wins in that time frame.

When you think that the Cardinals alone have had forty-nine managers to date in their history, it's remarkable that only two baseball managers have ever won the World Series with teams in both leagues—Tony LaRussa and Sparky Anderson.

Of course, it's more than this sterling list that earned LaRussa the Hall of Fame nod. Eight seasons managing the Chicago White Sox and ten seasons with the Oakland A's preceded his Cardinal era. Two of those seasons were split between teams.

Some may have forgotten that he won an American League pennant in his fourth full season in Chicago, winning 99 games and was major league Manager of the Year!

In Oakland there were four West Division championships, 1988-1990 and 1992. Of those, three seasons ended in the World Series. In 1989 the A's defeated the San Francisco Giants in the World Series, which was famously interrupted by the San Francisco earthquake.

So what are the characteristics that made this practicing attorney and animal crusader the third winningest manager (2,728) in the history of the game behind Connie Mack and John McGraw? It was a thirst for knowledge of the intricacies of the game.

In his book *Three Nights in August*, LaRussa reflected on how the game has changed over his forty years in baseball. "The growing importance of video, the decline of base stealing, the sharp drop in complete games by pitchers, the rise in home runs, and the biggest change, the way players think about the game."

LaRussa's intensity was unmatched. What is the appropriate strategy and play for every moment? He took losses hard and savored wins long enough to get to the next game. The layered complexities of baseball and all of its nuances fascinated, frustrated, and most of all challenged this great manager.

In his sixteen seasons in St. Louis, only three of those teams finished below third place. When he retired after the 2011 season, he was the longest tenured manager or head coach in any of the "big four" sports— baseball, basketball, football, and hockey.

Major League Baseball commissioner Bud Selig gave LaRussa a rarely awarded opportunity after No. 10 retired in 2011. Normally the current manager of the National League champion manages the All-Star Game, but in deference to his choice to retire, baseball asked LaRussa to manage the 2012 NL All-Stars instead of new Cardinals manager Mike Matheny. In his usual workmanlike way, he took the compliment and then guided the NL to a rare victory.

LaRussa had tendencies that were old school yet new school. He blended his baseball experience and instincts with the newfound metrics that lean on statistics and tendencies to make crucial in-game decisions. A passionate man in everything he attempts, whether it's winning a baseball game, raising money for a charity, or winning a round of golf, he's a Hall of Famer in every way.

The voters in Cooperstown nominated LaRussa for induction unanimously on December 9, 2013. He remains active off the field in the commissioner's office.

> *When he retired after the 2011 season, he was the longest tenured manager or head coach in any of the "big four" sports— baseball, basketball, football, and hockey.*

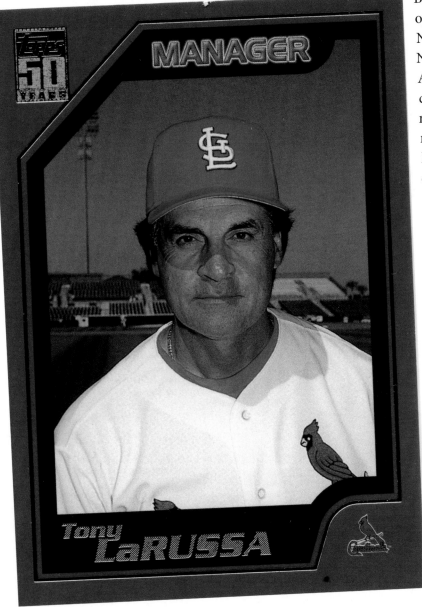

MANAGER

Tony LaRUSSA

JOHN McGRAW

Inducted in 1934 • Year with the Cardinals 1900

1899, 1901–1932	G	W	L	W-L%
33 Seasons	4769	2763	1948	.586

It could be said that John McGraw was the one the Cardinals let get away. He played just one season in St. Louis way back in 1900, after nine outstanding seasons beginning in 1891. He was a right-handed throwing third baseman and a hot-hitting left-hander who posted a lifetime .334 batting average, with on-base percentages mostly in the .450 to .510 range. Of course, McGraw wasn't elected to the Hall of Fame for his playing days; instead, it was his prowess as a manager from 1901 to 1932. For three seasons, he managed Baltimore, followed by his legendary tenure directing the New York Giants. McGraw, whose best-known nickname was Little Napoleon for his tongue lashings of players and umpires, was thrown out of a record 118 games over his career!

JOHN J. McGRAW
STAR THIRD-BASEMAN OF THE GREAT BALTIMORE ORIOLES, NATIONAL LEAGUE CHAMPIONS IN THE '90'S. FOR 30 YEARS MANAGER OF THE NEW YORK GIANTS STARTING IN 1902. UNDER HIS LEADERSHIP THE GIANTS WON 10 PENNANTS AND 3 WORLD CHAMPIONSHIPS.

That one year in St. Louis, he had come to the city under duress. His wife had died from a ruptured appendix, causing McGraw to miss the last month of the season in Baltimore. When the team then disbanded as the National League dropped to just eight teams, McGraw was sold to the Cardinals with a fellow teammate, catcher Wilbert Robinson (another future Hall of Famer). He wouldn't have reported to the Cards without signing baseball's largest contract, ten thousand dollars, after which he produced that .344 average in a season reduced to ninety-nine games, by both injuries and his penchant for getting ejected.

The team didn't fare well with McGraw. The Cardinals—owned by the Robison brothers—finished in fifth place, ten games under .500. He longed for Baltimore, expressed dissatisfaction with the city of St. Louis, and as the story goes, rode back to Baltimore after chucking his Cardinals uniform into the Mississippi River.

McGraw jockeyed around as a player-manager back with his Baltimore team in 1901 and part of 1902, but after the commissioner of the new American League, Ban Johnson, suspended him, McGraw grabbed six good players and jumped to the NL Giants for good.

He was miles ahead in game strategy, using pinch hitters and relief pitchers, and his players were aggressive on the bases. McGraw was a winner and a magnet for celebrities, politicians, and show-biz types. His Giants won four straight pennants from 1921 to 1924, with world championships over Babe Ruth's Yankees in 1921 and 1922. In all, he tallied 2,763 wins (second only to the dean of managers, Connie Mack of Philadelphia), ten pennants, and three world championships.

In the book *The Giants of the Polo Grounds*, author Noel Hynd summed up the measure of the little "big" man with a quote from McGraw: "In playing or managing, the game of ball is only fun for me when I'm out in front and winning. I don't give a hill of beans for the rest of the game."

John McGraw died of prostate cancer in 1934, and was inducted into the Hall of Fame in 1937.

BILL McKECHNIE

Inducted in 1962 • Years with the Cardinals 1928–1929

1915, 1922–1946	G	W	L	W-L%
25 Seasons	3647	1896	1723	.524

Another Hall of Famer with just a brief stint in St. Louis, Bill McKechnie made his mark in the dugout as a manager, not on the playing field. As a player, the Deacon—so named for his strict church-going habit—had a modest .251 career batting mark while playing third base for eight different ball clubs. What managers did see in McKechnie was a baseball mind, and by mid-season in 1922, he was managing full time for Pittsburgh.

In 1925 he won his first pennant and defeated the Washington Senators in the World Series. However, in a strange twist, he was fired in the 1926 season as the Pirates owner brought back the former manager as a front office consultant. The St. Louis Cardinals opened their doors to a coaching position after the 1927 season. Impatient Cardinal owner Sam Breadon replaced Bob O'Farrell with Bill McKechnie.

The Deacon was a mild-mannered gentleman who possessed a great analytical mind for managing. He inherited a powerful Redbird club. Hall of Famer Jim Bottomley was slugging away at first base while leading the league in home runs and RBIs. Second base star Frankie Frisch and outfielder Chick Hafey, plus 20-game-winner Jesse Haines, provided plenty of ammunition to win.

His team surged to a 95–59 record and returned to the World Series against the Yankees.

WILLIAM BOYD McKECHNIE
MANAGER OF
PITTSBURGH N.L. 1922·1926
ST. LOUIS N.L. 1928·1929
BOSTON N.L. 1930·1937
CINCINNATI N.L. 1938·1946
ONLY N.L. MANAGER TO WIN PENNANTS
WITH THREE DIFFERENT CLUBS·PITTSBURGH
1925; ST. LOUIS, 1928; CINCINNATI, 1939, 1940
WON WORLD SERIES 1925 AND 1940. NAMED
NO. 1 MAJOR LEAGUE MANAGER 1937 AND
1940. ACTIVE IN BASEBALL AS MANAGER,
COACH, PLAYER, 1906 TO 1953.

The Ruth-Gehrig combination was in high gear, and they whipped the Cards in the series, 4–0. The pasting didn't sit well with Breadon, and he demoted his manager to Triple-A Rochester, inserting future Hall of Famer Billy Southworth into the catbird's seat.

After eighty-eight games and in the middle of the league standings, McKechnie was brought back to St. Louis to manage, but the rest of the season didn't get much better. Painfully aware of the insecurity of the Cardinals' manager position, McKechnie took off for the Boston Braves, who offered him a long-term contract, and the Cardinals settled for their sixth manager in six seasons.

McKechnie coached eight years in Boston, nine years in Cincinnati, three in Cleveland as the third base coach, and a pair of seasons as the Boston Red Sox pitching coach. He led the 1939 Cincinnati Reds to 97 wins and a World Series against the Yankees. As an encore, those Reds won 100 games in 1940 and avenged their 1939 World Series loss by defeating the Detroit Tigers.

The Deacon has a special distinction shared by no other manager. He is the only one to have managed three different teams to the World Series: the Cardinals, Pittsburgh, and Cincinnati. He was inducted into the Hall of Fame in 1962 after winning 1,896 games in twenty-five seasons as a manager.

BRANCH RICKEY

Inducted in 1967 • Years with the Cardinals 1917–1942, 1963–1965

1913–1915, 1919–1925	G	W	L	W-L%
10 Seasons	1277	597	664	.473

Branch Rickey, known as the Professor of Baseball because of his experimental methods, undoubtedly had more influence on the game of baseball than any nonplayer in the history of the game. He made two notable contributions to Major League Baseball—creating the minor league system while serving as general manager of the St. Louis Cardinals, and integrating organized baseball when he signed Jackie Robinson to a contract with the Brooklyn Dodgers.

Rickey, however, meant much more to baseball. Wesley Branch Rickey, who excelled in sports and graduated with honors from Ohio Wesleyan University, had hopes of becoming a major league catcher. He had a strict religious upbringing on a farm in Lucasville, Ohio, which he maintained for the rest of his life. As an example, he was signed by the Cincinnati Reds but was dropped soon after because he refused to play on Sundays. He caught briefly for the St. Louis Browns and then the New York Yankees, but he appeared in only 120 games in three years, hitting a combined .239. He did put his name in the record books while catching for the Yankees,

WESLEY BRANCH RICKEY
ST. LOUIS A.L. 1905·1906·1914
NEW YORK A.L. 1907
FOUNDER OF FARM SYSTEM WHICH HE DEVELOPED FOR ST. LOUIS CARDINALS AND BROOKLYN DODGERS. COPIED BY ALL OTHER MAJOR LEAGUE TEAMS. SERVED AS EXECUTIVE FOR BROWNS, CARDINALS, DODGERS AND PIRATES. BROUGHT JACKIE ROBINSON TO BROOKLYN IN 1947.

when 13 Washington Senators players stole bases off him in one game.

His loss of a major league career as a player was still baseball's gain. He went to law school at the University of Michigan, but with baseball still running through his veins, he decided to accept an offer in 1912 to become the assistant to St. Louis Browns' owner Robert Lee Hedges, who had the insight to see that Rickey could bring with him a player's instinct, the wisdom of an attorney, and innovative thinking. Two years later, Hedges made Rickey the Browns' manager, a position he held until 1917 when he switched allegiances and became the Cardinals' field leader. He remained the Cardinals' manager until 1925 when he became the team's general manager, a position he held until 1942.

Under Rickey's guidance the Cardinals became one of the most successful franchises in the National League. The Cardinals needed good ballplayers to compete against the wealthiest NL teams. To compensate for his limited budget, Rickey created the farm system, a method of

Rickey (second from left) hams it up with Joe Medwick (left), Rip Collins (second from right), and Pepper Martin (right) while celebrating the twenty-fifth anniversary of the Gashouse Gang's championship season.

developing players at the minor league level. The system not only allowed players to develop their own talent, but it also gave the Cardinals a surplus of players who could be sold to other teams, thus helping

For the next two decades, Rickey's farm system produced many great players and kept the Cardinals in pennant contention.

the team's profit margin. Together with good scouts and Rickey's own judge of talent, the system worked. In the early 1930s, when the Depression was at its peak, the Cardinals signed any player with good batting skills, speed, and a good arm for as little as sixty dollars per month.

When World War II broke out, the Cardinals owned fifteen minor league clubs outright and had working agreements with several others. By 1926 the Cardinals had the talent to not only win their first NL pennant in thirty-nine years, but also to capture the World Series championship over the

Gussie Busch brought Rickey back to St. Louis as a consultant in 1962.

powerful New York Yankees. For the next two decades, Rickey's farm system produced many great players and kept the Cardinals in pennant contention.

However, by 1942 Rickey and Cardinals' owner Sam Breadon weren't seeing eye to eye. Rickey resigned from the team and became the general manager of the Brooklyn Dodgers, where he also instituted his minor league system. As the Dodgers began to climb in the standings, Rickey's popularity soared, even though his sermon-like speeches, often injected with biblical quotations, had New York sportswriters calling him the Deacon or Mahatma (after India's leader Mahatma Ghandi). But he was always shrewd in his evaluation of players.

In 1943 Rickey started on a new venture—to integrate baseball. With the approval of the Brooklyn board of directors, he sent scouts around the country to find the player who combined talent with the fortitude to withstand the fans' taunts and hatred as he crossed the color barrier. In 1945 Rickey signed Kansas City Monarchs shortstop Jackie Robinson, and on April 10, 1947, Robinson was promoted to the Dodgers.

In 1962 Rickey re-established ties with the Cardinals, serving as a consultant for the next three years, and in 1967 the Veterans Committee selected him for the Baseball Hall of Fame.

WILBERT ROBINSON

Inducted in 1945 • Year with the Cardinals 1900

1902, 1914–1931	G	W	L	W-L%
19 Seasons	2819	1399	1398	.500

Wilbert Robinson's nickname was Uncle Robbie, and he spent seventeen seasons (1886–1902) playing in the big leagues and another eighteen (1914–1931) managing the Brooklyn Robins (later Dodgers). During all that time, his only exposure to St. Louis was a less-than-auspicious year with the Cardinals in 1900, playing in only sixty games with 210 at-bats and a weak .248 average. He became a Cardinal only because the Baltimore team folded in 1899.

So Robinson makes this publication by only a nudge. His catching prowess gained him notoriety, which may have helped him become an astute manager. He was credited with helping to get the best out of pitchers like Joe McGinnity, Giants' great Rube Marquard, and a pair who also became Cardinals in their later years, Dazzy Vance and Burleigh Grimes, then with Robinson's Brooklyn club.

Championships followed him around. Baltimore won in 1894, 1895, and 1896 with Robinson catching. Then his managerial skills brought National League titles to Brooklyn in 1916 and 1920. Over his eighteen seasons, Brooklyn won 1,375 games and lost 1,341. However, they lost both times in the World Series, to the Boston Red Sox in 1916 and to the Cleveland Indians in 1920. He was involved in five more pennants as the pitching coach for his buddy, manager John McGraw, with the New York Giants from 1903 to 1913.

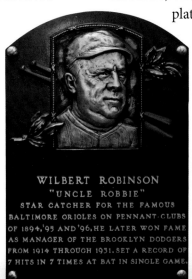

WILBERT ROBINSON
"UNCLE ROBBIE"
STAR CATCHER FOR THE FAMOUS
BALTIMORE ORIOLES ON PENNANT-CLUBS
OF 1894,'95 AND '96. HE LATER WON FAME
AS MANAGER OF THE BROOKLYN DODGERS
FROM 1914 THROUGH 1931. SET A RECORD OF
7 HITS IN 7 TIMES AT BAT IN SINGLE GAME.

Robinson had two other distinctive events during his baseball career. First, he is credited with being the first catcher in history to sit directly behind the plate at all times when other catchers would opt to play further back with less than two strikes on the batter. The second distinction relates to the Cardinals. Robinson set a baseball record while catching for the last-place Orioles against the St. Louis Browns (later Cardinals) on June 10, 1892. He went 7–7 at the plate with 11 runs batted in. His 7 hits in 7 at-bats in a game wasn't equaled until Rennie Stennett of the Pittsburgh Pirates tied it in 1975.

His 11 RBIs were eclipsed by a fellow Cardinal Hall of Famer. Ironically, Robinson was there the day it happened. In fact, he could have prevented it. Sunny Jim Bottomley drove in 12 runs against Robinson's Brooklyn team on September 16, 1924, as Robinson watched from the dugout. So why didn't he walk Bottomley when he got close to Robinson's record of 11 RBIs? The story goes he lost count and didn't realize Bottomley was so close!

Uncle Robbie got his nickname from the people in Brooklyn, and, in fact, that's how the Brooklyn team became "the Robins." He had a fun-loving personality, was thought to be a little absentminded at times, and the Brooklyn fans enjoyed his easygoing style of managing. He was inducted in the Baseball Hall of Fame in 1945.

BILLY SOUTHWORTH

Inducted in 2008 • Years with the Cardinals 1926–1927, 1929, 1940–1945

1929, 1940–1951	G	W	L	W-L%
13 Seasons	1770	1044	704	.597

Here is some noteworthy trivia. The St. Louis Cardinals have no less than eleven managers in Cooperstown! They are Roger Bresnahan, Roger Connor, Frank Frisch, Rogers Hornsby, Whitey Herzog, Miller Huggins, Bill McKechnie, Kid Nichols, Branch Rickey, Red Schoendienst, and Billy Southworth. Tony LaRussa will soon join them.

Billy Southworth could play baseball as well as manage a baseball team. The Harvard, Nebraska, native had a lifetime average of .298, playing from 1913 to 1929, including three years with the Cardinals: 1926, 1927, and 1929. As a player and manager, he was always around championships. Southworth was a contributor to the New York Giants' 1924 title and a key to the Cardinals' first world championship in 1926 as their regular right fielder. On September 24, 1926, he hit a two-run homer against the Giants to clinch the NL pennant for St. Louis. In the World Series, he went 10 for 29, with a double, triple, home run, six runs scored, and four RBIs.

By 1928 injury had made him a player-manager in the minor leagues. Although he appeared as a player-manager for the Cardinals in 1929, he spent the next decade managing in the minors. The Cardinals brought him back in 1940. General manager Branch Rickey had his minor league concept perking with players, and a budding superstar—Stan Musial—arrived in St. Louis. Musial became a "Southworth

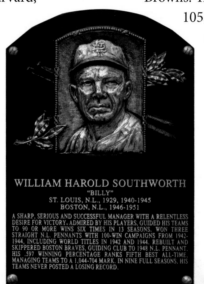

WILLIAM HAROLD SOUTHWORTH
"BILLY"
ST. LOUIS, N.L., 1929, 1940-1945
BOSTON, N.L., 1946-1951

A SHARP, SERIOUS AND SUCCESSFUL MANAGER WITH A RELENTLESS DESIRE FOR VICTORY. ADMIRED BY HIS PLAYERS, GUIDED HIS TEAMS TO 90 OR MORE WINS SIX TIMES IN 13 SEASONS. WON THREE STRAIGHT N.L. PENNANTS WITH 100-WIN CAMPAIGNS FROM 1942-1944, INCLUDING WORLD TITLES IN 1942 AND 1944. REBUILT AND SKIPPERED BOSTON BRAVES, GUIDING CLUB TO 1948 N.L. PENNANT. HIS .597 WINNING PERCENTAGE RANKS FIFTH BEST ALL-TIME. MANAGING TEAMS TO A 1,044-704 MARK. IN NINE FULL SEASONS, HIS TEAMS NEVER POSTED A LOSING RECORD.

disciple," giving Billy great credit for his early training. "Billy was a very good manager," said an admiring Musial. "He treated all of us young players fairly, and he really helped mold us into some great ball clubs."

The Cardinals won three straight NL pennants from 1942 to 1944. In 1942 they beat the New York Yankees, and in 1944 they won the classic Streetcar Series against the St. Louis Browns. Those powerhouses won 106, 105, and 105 games in those three seasons, which, to this day, is the most dominant era of Cardinals baseball.

His reputation was that of a no-nonsense taskmaster, but he was not at all unreasonable in his dealings with the players. He was innovative in some regards. Red Schoendienst, who also broke in as a player under Southworth, praised him. "Billy was a good man, and he liked to rely on his veterans to lead, like center fielder Terry Moore, who was our team captain. . . . He was innovative in that he was about the first manager who would pull a pitcher for a reliever in the eighth and ninth innings."

His three straight 100-win seasons remains a National League record. He managed thirteen seasons with a .597 winning percentage, fifth on the all-time list. He is first on the Cardinals' list at .642 with a 620–346 mark. In 2008 the Veterans Committee finally recognized Southworth's contributions to baseball and elected him into the Baseball Hall of Fame.

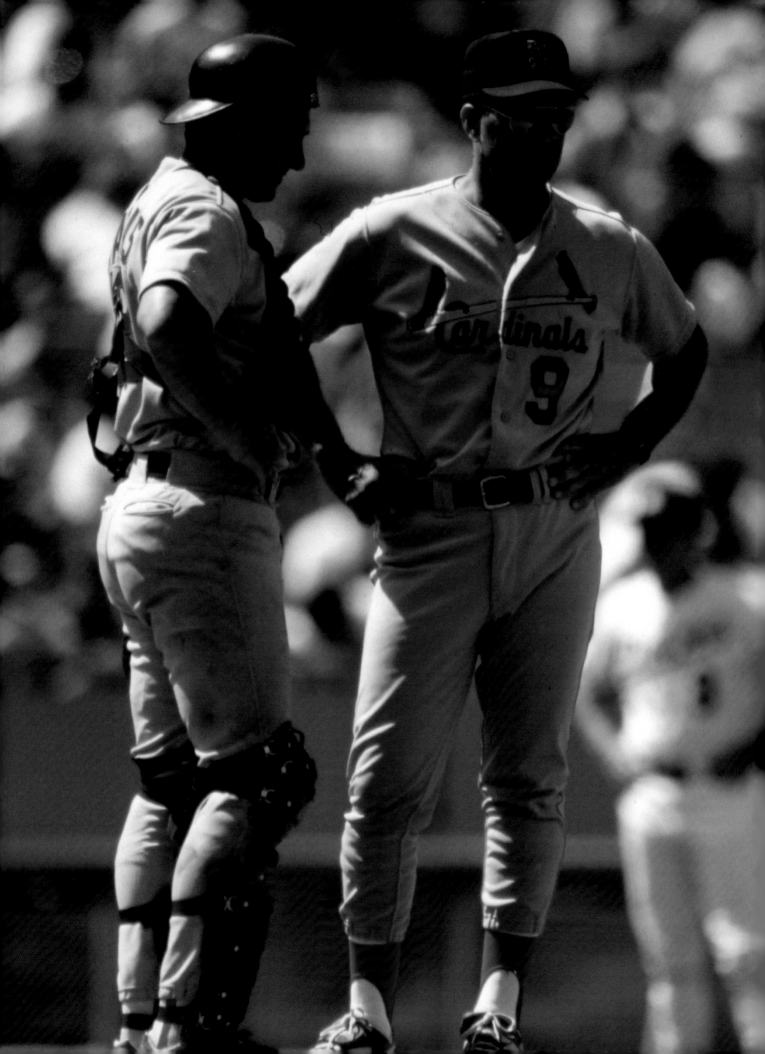

JOE TORRE

Inducted in 2014 • Years with the Cardinals 1990–1995

1977–1984, 1990–2010	G	W	L	W-L%
29 Seasons	4323	2326	1997	.538

Today's fans know Joe Torre as a Hall of Fame manager with five teams, but all of his 10 American League East Division titles, six pennants, and four World Series championships came with the New York Yankees. His Cardinals seasons produced three winning records, in 1992, 1993, and 1994, but by 1995 his efforts and that of his buddy and general manager Dal Maxvill were being severely hindered by a disinterested ownership in Anheuser-Busch.

Joe, of course, went on to build his Cooperstown resume in New York, but his real contribution to St. Louis was on the field. After eight solid seasons with the Milwaukee and then Atlanta Braves, the Cardinals acquired Torre in 1969 in a trade for the 1967 most valuable player, Orlando Cepeda. Little did they know it would end up being "one MVP for another"!

Torre's credentials were well known. Called up as a rookie in May 1961 for injured All-Star catcher Del Crandall, and with few expectations right away, Torre hit .278 with 21 doubles and 10 home runs. He finished second to the Cubs' Billy Williams for the National League Rookie of the Year.

His career took off from there. Installed as the starting catcher in '63, he hit .293, with 14 homers and 71 RBIs, and won a reserve spot on the All-Star team. Torre would earn nine All-Star

Game selections, four times in St. Louis—1970, 1971, 1972, and 1973.

Joe was happy with the trade in 1969, coming without great pressure, as the Cardinals had Lou Brock, Curt Flood, Tim McCarver, and Richie Allen for their power. It allowed Torre to get comfortable in the surroundings and emerge as a team leader in 1970 when Allen was traded and he became the full-time third baseman.

His numbers spoke for themselves in 1970. He bashed 21 homers, had 100 RBIs and hit .325, second in the National League. With McCarver the entrenched starting catcher, Torre's energy wasn't sapped and his hitting increased.

His 1971 achievements earned him the cover of *Sports Illustrated* for the April 1972 Baseball Preview edition. He posted a .363 batting average with 137 RBIs and 230 hits, leading the NL in all three categories. Interestingly, he hit .363 against right-handers and .362 against left-handers.

Torre was named the National League's Most Valuable Player. The Cardinals won 90 and lost 72, finishing second for manager Red Schoendienst. Torre was a team leader with Brock and Bob Gibson, a trait that set him up nicely for his future managerial and then baseball administrative career.

"I didn't bust watercoolers or throw bats, but

I did root and holler on the bench if I thought the team was getting down on each other," said Joe in the 1972 *Sports Illustrated* story. "Bob Gibson gave me some good advice one evening in Philadelphia after I had popped up in my third at-bat after getting two hits my first two times up. I was steaming on the bench trying to show my emotions to my teammates when he said, 'You expect to get a hit everytime up?'

"I said I did and Bob put his finger to his mouth and said, 'Shhh, even I can't do that.' He taught me a lot about being competitive and in control."

Not surprisingly, Torre won the Hutch Award after his '71 season, given annually to the player who best exemplifies the fighting spirit and competitive

Torre was a team leader with Brock and Bob Gibson, a trait that set him up nicely for his future managerial and then baseball administrative career.

desire of the late, great manager Fred Hutchinson. He had Cardinal ties as their manager from 1956 to 1958.

In eighteen seasons as a player, Torre totaled 2,209 games, 2,342 hits, 252 home runs, 1,185 RBIs, an on-base percentage of .365, and fielding stats of .990 as a catcher, .993 at first base, and .951 at third base. He hit over .300 and had over 100 RBIs five times and earned one Gold Glove as a catcher. He had no postseason appearances.

Again, it was his managerial accomplishments that earned his Hall of Fame nomination. Overall, he compiled a .605 winning percentage with 2,326 wins, fifth all-time.

Recognizing his incredible leadership skills, Commissioner Bud Selig wanted Torre on the Major League Baseball staff immediately upon his retirement from managing. He was appointed executive vice president for baseball operations, interrupted briefly by an aborted attempt by a group he was in to buy the Los Angeles Dodgers.

Torre was selected as the manager of the USA team in the 2013 World Baseball Classic, and was inducted into the St. Louis Sports Hall of Fame in 2013.

Finally, he was nominated for induction into Cooperstown by the Veterans Committee in 2014.

ST. LOUIS
CARDINALS
1991
MEDIA GUIDE
$6.00

BILL VEECK

Inducted in 1991 • Years as an Owner of the Browns 1951–1953

If Bill Veeck entered the circus business instead of the world of baseball, Barnum & Bailey would have been relegated to a second-string outfit.

A consummate showman, Veeck's promotions with three major league teams were so outrageous, even the showmen of the three-ring circus spectacles would have been astounded. From sending a midget up to bat or using a clown (Max Patkin) as a first base coach when he was owner of the St. Louis Browns to Disco Demolition Night when he owned the Chicago White Sox, Veeck continually thought up promotions that rocked the world of Major League Baseball.

Exploding scoreboards, fireworks displays, bat days, names on the backs of uniforms, shorts for his ballplayers' uniforms, and even involving fans in managerial decision-making, prompted the title of his autobiography, *Veeck as in Wreck*.

BILL VEECK
OWNER OF INDIANS, BROWNS AND WHITE SOX. CREATED HEIGHTENED FAN INTEREST AT EVERY STOP WITH INGENIOUS PROMOTIONAL SCHEMES, FAN PARTICIPATION, EXPLODING SCOREBOARD, OUTRAGEOUS DOOR PRIZES, NAMES ON UNIFORMS. SET M.L. ATTENDANCE RECORD WITH PENNANT-WINNER AT CLEVELAND IN 1948; WON AGAIN WITH 'GO-GO' SOX IN 1959. SIGNED A.L.'S FIRST BLACK PLAYER, LARRY DOBY IN 1947 AND OLDEST ROOKIE, 42 YEAR OLD SATCHEL PAIGE IN 1948.
A CHAMPION OF THE LITTLE GUY.

William Lewis Veeck Jr., without a doubt the most innovative owner and inveterate hustler in baseball history, was the son of a baseball writer who was so knowledgeable about the sport that William Wrigley appointed him president of the Chicago Cubs. That gave young Bill his entree into baseball. He worked in concessions and even helped the groundskeepers. When his father died in 1933, he left college to work full-time for the Cubs.

Several years later, at age 27, he purchased the Milwaukee franchise in the American Association, taking the team from near bankruptcy to one of the most profitable in the league. His team, mainly through his promotional wizardry, set attendance records. His promotions sometimes weren't announced beforehand, and he gave away pigs and food and put on fireworks displays. Four years later, he sold the club for a $275,000 profit.

In his book, he admitted that he almost purchased the Philadelphia Phillies in 1943 with thoughts of signing some Negro League players. But fearing a fan backlash, he backed off the deal, a move he said he later regretted. But in 1946, after the amputation of a leg (the result of wounds suffered fighting in the South Pacific with the Marines in World War II), he bought the Cleveland Indians. His promotions helped to double attendance within a year and to set a then league attendance record of 2,670,627 in 1947 when Cleveland won the pennant.

He signed the first black player in the AL, Larry Doby, and later inked Satchel Paige, who became the oldest major league rookie at age forty-two. He again made a huge profit when he sold the Indians.

In 1951 he bought the hapless St. Louis Browns, a team highly in debt. A year later, Veeck used every promotion his inventive mind could conjure up.

Those gimmicks were priceless. Like when he put the ageless Paige in a rocking chair. Or when, on August 24, 1951, Veeck staged Grandstand

Manager Day. A day before, he held a contest in the *St. Louis Globe-Democrat* that would allow fans to vote on the Browns' starting lineup. Everyone who mailed in his ballot received a ticket to the Browns–Philadelphia Athletics game. Veeck placed them in a special section behind the Browns dugout called the Grandstand Managers Section. They actually voted on what plays the Browns should do next. A sign was held up above the Browns dugout asking the crowd what they would like the Browns to do. Then, the crowd would quickly hold up a green sign for "yes" or a red sign for "no." The 1,115 "managers," proved mostly right in the Browns' 5–3 victory.

But Veeck's most notable stunt was sending up a midget to bat. Between games of a doubleheader with Detroit on August 19, 1951, Veeck signed Eddie Gaedel, who was 3′7″ and weighed 65 pounds.

In his book, Veeck wrote: "Eddie came to us in a moment of desperation. Not his desperation, ours. After a month or so in St. Louis, we were looking around desperately for a way to draw a few people into the ball park, it being perfectly clear by that time that the ball club wasn't going to do it unaided."

Veeck sought an athletic midget actor and, a month before the event, talked Gaedel into going to bat for the Browns. He coached Gaedel into a squatting batting stance to give him a smaller strike zone. "When Eddie went into that crouch, his strike zone was just about visible to the naked eye," Veeck said. "I picked up a ruler and measured it for posterity. It was 1½ inches."

Gaedel's "performance" was a secret to all but a few. All the fans knew was that something special was planned for the doubleheader. Veeck had Gaedel use the uniform of seven-year-old Bill DeWitt Jr., a Browns' batboy at the time and future owner of the St. Louis Cardinals. Veeck had the number ⅛ put on the jersey and in the program.

Between games, Gaedel popped out of a birthday cake intended for manager Zack Taylor, who was in on the gimmick. But the fun was only beginning. In the bottom half of the first inning, Gaedel emerged from the dugout waving three little bats. "Now batting for the Browns," said the PA announcer,

Perhaps Bill Veeck's greatest stunt in baseball was sending midget Eddie Gaedel up to bat for the Browns on August 19, 1951.

"number one-eighth, Eddie Gaedel."

Eddie Hurley, the umpire behind the plate, took one look at Gaedel and started toward the Browns' dugout. Taylor showed the umpire Gaedel's contract and a telegram to headquarters, verifying he was indeed a player. The stadium went wild. Bobby Cain was the Detroit pitcher, and Bob Swift was the catcher. Swift rose to the occasion by getting down on both knees to offer his pitcher a target.

Cain started out by really trying to pitch to Gaedel, who stood more upright than Veeck had planned. Still, Cain's first two deliveries were high. By the third pitch, Cain was laughing so hard that he could barely throw. Ball three and ball four sailed about three feet over Eddie's head.

Eddie trotted down to first base waving his cap and bowing to the crowd. Jim Delsing then came in as a pinch runner. It was a gag that went down in the annals of Major League Baseball.

The next day, AL president Will Harridge issued an executive order barring Gaedel from baseball. A new rule was promptly passed making it mandatory that all player contracts be filed with and approved by the president.

Meanwhile, Veeck was stockpiling talent to boost the lineup—players such as Virgil Trucks, Vic Wertz, Clint Courtney, Johnny Groth, and Paige. Along with holdover personnel such as Roy Sievers, Bob Turley, and Don Larsen, the Browns' outlook was good. But when financially rich Anheuser-Busch purchased the Cardinals in 1953, Veeck decided St. Louis couldn't support two teams.

He planned to move the Browns to Milwaukee, but the National League outmaneuvered Veeck and moved the Boston Braves there. Next Veeck set his sights on Baltimore, but the AL voted him down. Veeck said he felt the other owners colluded to keep him in St. Louis in an effort to bankrupt him because they didn't agree with his outlandish methods. When he sold the team to Clarence Miles, a Baltimore attorney, the same owners quickly voted to allow the move to Baltimore.

Veeck tried several ventures after that, including trying to buy the Ringling Brothers circus, and in 1959 he headed a group that purchased the White

Sox. But on advice from his doctors, he sold the club.

However, he couldn't stay away from baseball and returned to buy the White Sox in 1979. It was in Chicago that he promoted Disco Demolition Night on July 12, 1979, during which fans burned disco records in a huge bonfire on the field between games of a twi-night doubleheader at Comiskey Park. The field became such a mess afterwards that umpire Dave Phillips deemed it unplayable and forfeited the second game to the Tigers.

"As we emerged from the umpires' dressing room expecting to start the second game, there were thousands of fans on the field and portions of the outfield in center field were in flames because of a radio station–sponsored promotion gone haywire," Phillips said. "In fact I wrote a book titled *Center Field On Fire*—and it really was."

Five years later, after buying the club for $7 million, he sold the White Sox for $20 million.

A heavy smoker and light beer drinker, Veeck gave up both in 1980 and underwent two operations for lung cancer in 1984. He died from the disease on January 2, 1986, at the age of seventy-one. He was elected to the Baseball Hall of Fame five years later.

ST. LOUIS CARDINALS 1944

Summary
NL St. Louis Cardinals (4) vs. AL St. Louis Browns (2)

Game	Score	Date
1	Browns 2, Cardinals 1	October 4
2	Cardinals 3, Browns 2 (11 innings)	October 5
3	Browns 6, Cardinals 2	October 6
4	Cardinals 5, Browns 1	October 7
5	Cardinals 2, Browns 0	October 8
6	Cardinals 3, Browns 1	October 9

With World War II raging in 1944, the player pool in the major leagues was severely reduced as many of the league's performers were called to arms. But in St. Louis there was just enough talent to result in the first—and only—all–St. Louis World Series.

The Browns had to win 11 of their last 12 games to capture their only American League pennant. Even then, they did so with a rather depleted cast. In fact, the Browns sported only one .300 hitter and Mike Kreevich barely made that at .301.

Meanwhile, St. Louis needed two home runs by Chet Laabs on the final day of the regular season, giving the Browns a four-game series sweep over the defending champion New York Yankees. Detroit, meanwhile, sealed its own doom by losing it's final game of the season to Washington, enabling the Browns to win the pennant by that one game over the Tigers.

The Cardinals, meanwhile, won their third consecutive National League pennant by 14½ games over Pittsburgh. Needless to say the Cardinals were heavy favorites to win what was billed as the Streetcar Series or the St. Louis Showdown at Sportsman's Park.

With excitement raging among St. Louis fans the series opened on October 6, and the Browns' Denny Galehouse outpitched 22-game winner Mort Cooper. Behind Galehouse and George McQuinn's fourth-inning, two-run homer, the Browns posted a 2–1 victory in Game 1.

Game 2 featured great relief pitching from the Cardinals' Blix Donnelly and when Ken O'Dea stroked a run-scoring pinch single in the eleventh inning, the Redbirds had tied the series at one game apiece and it looked like a series that would be close all the way through.

The Browns came back to take a 2–1 series lead in Game 3 when Jack Kramer allowed only seven hits, while striking out 10. His teammates scored four runs in the third inning off Ted Wilkes as the AL team posted a 6–2 victory.

But it was all Cardinals from there.

Behind southpaw Harry "The Cat" Brecheen, who recorded a 16–5 regular-season record, and a two-run homer by 23-year-old Stan Musial, the Redbirds evened the series with a 5–1 victory. The next day, Cooper, who won 65 games (including 23 shutouts) the previous three seasons, avenged his first-game loss to Galehouse with a seven-hit, 2–0 shutout victory. Both Redbird runs came on home runs—by Danny Litwhiler and Ray Sanders.

Game 6 matched the two teams' aces—16-game winner Max Lanier for the Cardinals and Nels Potter, who went 19–7 in '44. Lanier, with relief help from Wilks, another 16-game winner, prevailed. The pair ended the Browns' Cinderella season, as the Redbirds posted a three-run fourth inning against Potter for a 3-1 victory. The victory gave the Cards their second world championship in three years.

"The funny thing about that World Series," Musial said later, "was that the fans were rooting for the Browns, and it kind of surprised me because we drew more fans than the Browns during the season. . . . But after you analyze the situation in St. Louis, the Browns in the old days had good clubs. They had great players like George Sisler and Kenny Williams, and the fans who were there were older fans, older men, old-time Brownie fans. But it was a tough series."

And it was the Cardinals who survived in the end.

ST. LOUIS IN THE NEGRO NATIONAL LEAGUE

1922-1931

In 1910 a black Cuban baseball team called the Havana Stars played a six-game series against the Detroit Tigers. It ended in a 3–3 tie. Commissioner Kenesaw Mountain Landis was furious and banned Major League Baseball teams from playing black baseball teams for fear of embarrassment.

Ten years later, in 1920, a man named Andrew Rube Foster called a meeting at the Kansas City YMCA and formed the Negro National League. In the same year, a 29-year-old superstar pitcher, John Donaldson, moved from J.L Wilkinson's All Nations team to the Kansas City Monarchs. In fact, it is thought that Donaldson came up with the name Monarchs for this new black baseball team.

The St. Louis Giants had existed since 1906 as an independent, like teams in most cities, before joining the new Negro National League in 1920. The Giants had a stadium, a white investor, and a core of good players. They were good enough to win the local St. Louis City League championship in 1912 and 1913.

They played two more seasons. In 1920 the team finished in sixth place with a record of 25–32, a down year as they adapted to the new competition in the NNL. The acquisition of Oscar Charleston, who hit .436 with 12 home runs, triggered a season of 40 wins and 28 losses, good for second place.

The Giants' high point was a best-of-seven series at Sportsman's Park against the St. Louis Cardinals. The Giants got beat four games to one. That winter the ownership changed hands.

They had run out of funding with poor attendance, and were sold by African American promoter Charlie Mills to Dick Kent and Dr. Sam Sheppard.

The team was renamed the St. Louis Stars and a new stadium was built at the southwest corner of Market St. and Compton Ave., across from what is now the Chaifetz Arena of St. Louis University.

The team's struggles continued until they got a break in 1923 when the Toledo Tigers folded and their best talent went to St. Louis for new manager Candy Jim Taylor. He was a player-manager at age thirty-seven, who had swatted 20 home runs in 1923.

Taylor could judge talent and he built the Stars into a dynasty. Cool Papa Bell, Willie Wells, Mule Suttles, and pitcher Ted Trent combined for a winning formula.

The Stars, playing at their 10,000-seat Stars Park, one of the best in the league, became a power. They won league championships in 1928, 1930, and 1931. St. Louis had two championship baseball teams at the same time. But even though the stadiums of the Stars and Cardinals were separated by a mere two miles, they may have well been a thousand miles apart due to the racial segregation of the time.

The NNL didn't play nearly as many games as major league teams and it didn't consistently play the same number of games each year, thus making it difficult to compare statistics between the Negro National League and the major leagues.

But what can't be denied is the talent of the players who were prohibited from playing with the all-white major leagues. It would have been a golden era if Josh Gibson, Cool Papa Bell, and other stars of the Negro National League could have faced off against Rogers Hornsby, Ty Cobb, and Honus Wagner!

Integration in those days would have significantly advanced the game's quality and given so many more men their just due. The Stars and the Negro League itself disbanded at the end of the 1931 season.

CHAPTER 8

MEDIA

Just as the Cardinals employed so many Hall of Fame–caliber ballplayers over the years, so too has the St. Louis public been blessed to read the descriptions of the games and get the inside stories of the players from sportswriters and broadcasters who could entertain and enlighten with the stroke of their pen or the inflection of

their voice. In the highly competitive arena of baseball reporting, in an era of unprecedented numbers of reporters, sports radio hosts, television commentators, and online analysts, it's hard to stand out. In the Hall of Fame, sportswriters are awarded the J.G. Taylor Spink Award, while broadcasters are awarded the Ford C. Frick Award.

BOB BROEG
J.G. Taylor Spink Award Winner 1979

There will not be another sportswriter in St. Louis whose impact locally and nationally will exceed that of the late Robert William Patrick Broeg. He lived when the newspaper was king of the media. Whether it was through the written word in his *St. Louis Post-Dispatch* columns or the spoken word at a banquet, radio show, TV show, or just in conversation, the never-brief Broeg could mesmerize his audience with tantalizing words that would make them feel part of the story.

A postwar hire at the *Post-Dispatch*, Broeg spent forty years covering his beloved baseball Cardinals on the beat from 1945 to 1958, and his second favorite, the black and gold of Old Mizzou. He became the contributing sports editor in 1958 and held the position until 1985. He possessed a bellowing voice and never backed down. Many young scribes flocked for advice, and the kind, passionate Broeg would treat each like a son.

An eye injury at birth hampered his own playing ability, but it didn't keep him from spending hours with the great stars of sports from Babe Ruth and Ty Cobb to his favorite, Stan Musial. It's said he had much to do with the nickname of Musial—that unforgettable Stan the Man comment Broeg heard resonating from the crowd in Brooklyn's Ebbets Field.

He made a real contribution to the game of baseball and its players when he helped create and push through the first pension program for veteran major league ballplayers. There were many down-and-out players who needed help from the game that they had done so much to make great. He fought for the Hall of Fame election of Cardinals stars. In particular, he championed the causes of Red Schoendienst,

Chick Hafey, and Enos Slaughter.

Broeg had his fingers in many sports. He had great knowledge of the boxing world, shared his time covering the St. Louis Football Cardinals, and followed closely the exploits of his good friend Ben Kerner, who owned the St. Louis Hawks of the NBA. He was published in many places, including the *Sporting News* and the *Saturday Evening Post*. He wrote some twenty-four books about the topics he loved. A great stats man as well, Broeg had the honor of having the St. Louis chapter of the Society for American Baseball Research named for him.

He was very influential in Cooperstown. Broeg was a member of the board of directors of the Hall of Fame and became a senior member of the Hall of Fame's Veterans Committee.

When he died in October 2005, his funeral was attended by baseball and sports dignitaries from all over. Among them was the president of the Baseball Hall of Fame in Cooperstown. Greg Marecek—coauthor of this book—was honored to be a speaker, and in his eulogy he said fondly and with great sadness, "This day Bob Broeg is busy writing for the *Heavenly Post*."

There will never be a time again when a sportswriter can have the influence, the audience, and the freedom to become such an institution to his constituents. Broeg's name and face are proudly displayed by the St. Louis Cardinals on the door of the Bob Broeg–Rick Hummel Press Box.

His list of awards is endless, but his greatest achievement and source of pride was being awarded the J.G. Taylor Spink Award and being inducted into the baseball writers' wing of the National Baseball Hall of Fame in 1980.

JACK BUCK

Ford C. Frick Award Winner 1987

His deep, gravelly voice was easily recognizable, not only to the St. Louis Cardinals audience, but to the nation as well. He was skillful with the spoken word, and his quick wit enthralled the Cardinal audience.

For almost five decades Jack Buck was the voice of the Cardinals, teaming first with Harry Caray and Joe Garagiola in 1954 and completing his tenure with former Cardinal Mike Shannon in the radio booth. In between, his low-key style was heard on CBS radio where he covered eight World Series, seventeen Super Bowls, and four major league All-Star Games.

Many of his calls are memorable. Most notable to the St. Louis audience was his call in Game 5 of the NL Championship Series against the Dodgers when he exclaimed, "Go crazy folks, go crazy," after the light-hitting Ozzie Smith smacked a walk-off home run. Or Jack Clark's three-run homer two days later in Los Angeles in the top of the ninth in Game 6: "Adios! Goodbye! And maybe that's a winner!" Or describing Mark McGwire's 61st home run to tie Roger Maris's record: " Pardon me for a moment while I stand and applaud!" And of course, his signature call of "That's a winner," when the Cardinals won a game.

Buck's calls, however, were also noted nationwide. For instance, while broadcasting the "Ice Bowl" in 1967 between the Green Bay Packers and Dallas Cowboys, he asked the listeners to "Excuse me while I take a bite of my coffee." There was also his description of lame-legged Kirk Gibson's pinch-hit home run in the 1988 World Series: "I don't believe what I just saw."

John Francis "Jack" Buck was born in Massachusetts, the third of seven children, and was a Boston Red Sox fan. As a teen, among other odd jobs, he worked as a deckhand on iron ore boats. He was drafted into the army at age nineteen and suffered arm and leg injuries while crossing a bridge into Germany. While recuperating in a hospital, he received the Purple Heart. Upon his return he attended Ohio State University, majoring in radio speech and broadcasting for the campus radio station. "When I went on the air to do a sports show at WOSU, I had never done a sports show before," Buck wrote in his autobiography, *That's a Winner*. "When I did a basketball game, it was the first time I ever did play-by-play. The same with football. I didn't know how to do these things. I just did them."

Upon leaving school in 1953, he got a job broadcasting the baseball games of the Cardinals' minor league affiliate in Rochester, New York, then got the call to join Caray, Garagiola, and Milo Hamilton on the major league broadcasts in 1954. When Caray was fired in 1969, Buck took over as lead play-by-play man on the broadcasts. Shannon joined him in the booth in 1972, the beginning of a twenty-eight-year partnership.

Buck also announced football Cardinals games in the 1970s and 1980s and the inaugural

St. Louis Blues games. The ever-busy Buck also worked Monday Night Football games from 1978 through 1995 with Hank Stram, and did NBA and college basketball games, professional bowling, boxing, and wrestling at various times during his career.

While broadcasting the "Ice Bowl" in 1967 between the Green Bay Packers and Dallas Cowboys, he asked the listeners to "Excuse me while I take a bite of my coffee."

Buck is also remembered fondly for an original poem he read on one of his final public appearances. Several days after the tragic September 11 terrorist attacks, Buck recited his original writing when Major League Baseball resumed. Looking rather frail while struggling with obvious signs of Parkinson's disease and cancer, Buck brought the Busch Stadium crowd to tears with his emotional patriotic prose that he read during pre-game ceremonies.

Buck was awarded the Ford C. Frick Award from the Baseball Hall of Fame in 1987. He is also a member of the Football and Radio Halls of Fame.

One of baseball's all-time best broadcasting teams, Jack Buck and former Cardinals outfielder and third baseman Mike Shannon, pose in the broadcast booth.

Left: Lou Brock and Buck get a laugh at one of many postseason dinners.

HARRY CARAY
Ford C. Frick Award Winner 1989

If there is one word that describes the way Harry Caray broadcast baseball games, it's "unpredictable." Fanatical for the game, the fans, and the teams he announced, the charismatic play-by-play announcer wasn't afraid to express his feelings—and whatever else was on his mind—over the airways. Perhaps that's why his radio listeners hung on his every word as he brought major league baseball to life in households across the country.

Caray filled the St. Louis airways with his raucous, opinionated style for twenty-five years—a style that provided him with a huge following, but also made for many detractors. He enjoyed his role as lead broadcaster for the games, but his overwhelming personality was too much for some of those who worked alongside him.

Caray, who was born Harry Christopher Carabina, grew up in St. Louis and lived with an aunt and then in several foster homes after his parents died before he was ten years old. As a teenager he enjoyed playing sports and even envisioned playing with the Cardinals someday. When he realized he didn't have the talent to make it to the big leagues, he formed another idea. While a salesman for a company that made basketball backboards, he enjoyed listening to Cardinals games when he couldn't sneak away to attend the games. However, he didn't think the announcer was very exciting. In his autobiography, *Holy Cow*, he said he wrote to the general manager of KMOX-AM Radio, saying he felt the broadcasts were as "dull and boring as the morning crop reports." The general manager told Caray to get some experience and see if he could do better.

Thus, Caray took his distinctive style and started broadcasting games, first in Joliet, Illinois, and then in Kalamazoo, Michigan. He was then hired by the Cardinals in 1945 to broadcast their games on WIL-AM Radio, but the station manager told him that he would have to shorten his name. He turned Carabina into Caray, the name people would know him by for the rest of his life.

Caray moved to KMOX-AM when Anheuser-Busch, Inc., acquired the Cardinals ten years later, and he eventually partnered with Joe Garagiola and Jack Buck, among others. Now Caray could be heard throughout the country on more than 175 affiliated stations. The sounds of his favorite expression, "Holy Cow," when a great play was made, or his call of "It might be, it could be . . . it is a home run" became synonymous with listening to a Cardinals game.

At times, Caray broadcast shirtless from the bleachers, complete with beer cooler, and also used a long fishing net to catch foul balls from the press box.

Fans appreciated his candid on-air comments, which ranged from pure "homerism" to caustic remarks when a player made an error. But Caray didn't feel like he favored the home team. "When I'm at the ball park broadcasting a game, I'm the eyes and ears for that fan at home," he wrote in his book.

However, Caray fell out of favor with Cardinals management and was fired in 1969. One report said a scandalous affair with an executive's wife led to the termination, while others claimed it was his no-nonsense style of broadcasting. After his firing, Caray spent a year broadcasting Oakland A's games, then spent the next twenty-seven years in Chicago—eleven with the White Sox and sixteen with the Cubs. He gained nationwide attention with the Cubs when he appeared on superstation WGN.

The "Mayor of Rush Street" quickly became iconic. Caray initiated the stadium singing of "Take Me Out to the Ballgame" during the seventh-inning stretch of Chicago home games. "I would always sing it, because I think it's the only song I knew the words to!" he said. One day the engineer opened his microphone while he was singing, and the seventh-inning stretch became a little more interesting.

Caray received the Ford C. Frick Award from the Baseball Hall of Fame in 1989. He died as a result of cardiac arrest in 1998. His late son, Skip, and grandson, Chip, followed in his baseball broadcasting footsteps.

Right: Harry Caray enjoys an off-season ski trip in the Swiss Alps with public relations executive Bill Fisher, 1957.

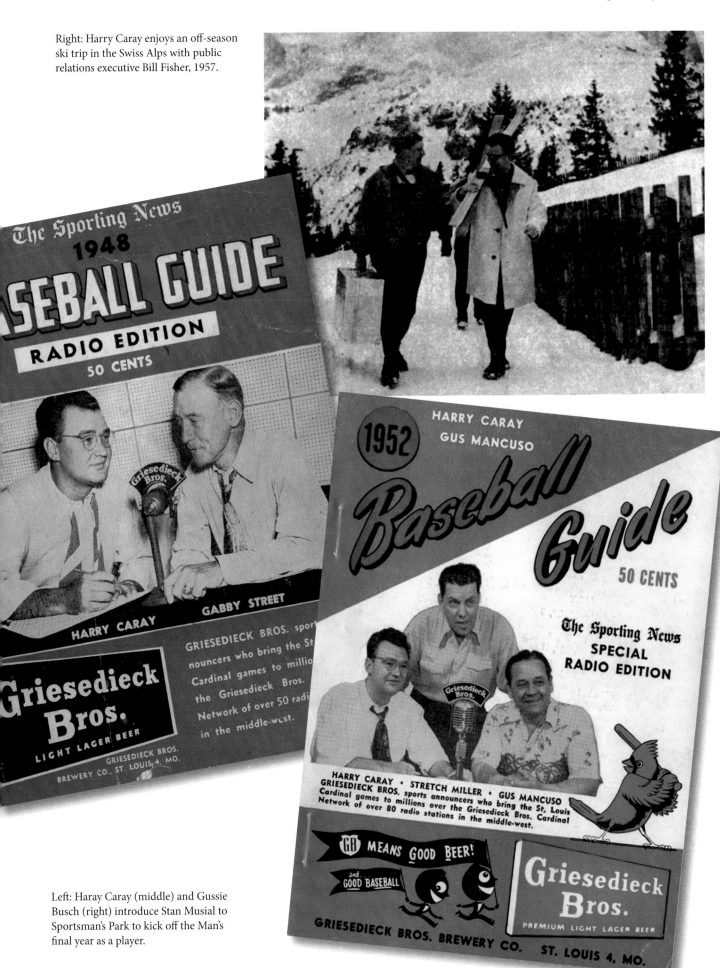

Left: Haray Caray (middle) and Gussie Busch (right) introduce Stan Musial to Sportsman's Park to kick off the Man's final year as a player.

JOE GARAGIOLA

Ford C. Frick Award Winner 1991

St. Louis born and bred and best pal of Yogi Berra from the Hill neighborhood in South St. Louis, Joe Garagiola was a fine baseball player before he progressed up the broadcast ladder to become one of the greats. He broke into baseball in 1946 with the St. Louis Cardinals, just in time to be on a world championship team. It would be his only experience with a championship on the field.

In that 1946 World Series against the Boston Red Sox, the hometown guy played in five games, batted .316 with four runs batted in, and played an important role in a Cardinal victory. In Game 4, Joe went 4 for 5, drove in three runs, and the Birds won in a rout, 12–3.

Garagiola spent nine seasons in the major leagues as a catcher, six of them with the Cardinals, but he made his mark on the game in the broadcast booth. Joe got his first break in broadcasting when the Cardinals' main man, Harry Caray, took a liking to him. It was Caray's urging that convinced Garagiola to retire from baseball and take up broadcasting. It was a novelty in those days for a former player to turn broadcaster, so Joe was a pioneer of sorts, and a really good one. He actually got his first break on television when Jack Buck's daughter, Christine, was hurt while horseback riding and the TV station needed one of the radio guys to move over and do the game while Jack went to the hospital.

Garagiola was on the Cardinals broadcast team from 1955 to 1962 as the second man to Caray. Jack Buck was there as well. Joe gained popularity with his self-deprecating stories and dry humor. He told a story about himself that he knew it was time to retire from baseball when his ex-teammate Stan Musial was standing in the batter's box, looked back at Garagiola catching for the Giants, and said, "So when are you going to quit?"

In 1961 he was already doing games for NBC in New York, a relationship that lasted for thirty years. He not only did baseball, but he also did six years on *The Today Show* (1967–1973) and game shows including *To Tell the Truth*, *Memory Game*, and *Sale of the Century*. He also did Monday Night Baseball's pre-game show called "The Baseball World of Joe Garagiola." Garagiola gained national notoriety on the Baseball Game of the Week with color commentator Tony Kubek, the former Yankees' star shortstop. Joe alternated games with Curt Gowdy until 1976 and stayed until Bob Costas arrived in 1983. Joe teamed up with Vin Scully in 1983, and the pair became the marquee baseball broadcasters in the 1980s, including three World Series—1984, 1986, and 1988.

Italian Joe always had a catchy phrase, much like his childhood friend Yogi Berra, who grew up with Garagiola on Elizabeth Avenue on the Hill. When he and Yogi were recruited, Garagiola was rated the better baseball prospect. It didn't turn out that way, and Joe liked to crack, "Not only was I not the best catcher in the big leagues, I wasn't even the best catcher on my street!"

Major League Baseball's Hall of Fame voters chose to honor Joe Garagiola with the Ford C. Frick Award for outstanding baseball broadcasting accomplishments in 1991.

RICK HUMMEL

J.G. Taylor Spink Award Winner 2007

The rich sportswriting tradition of the *St. Louis Post-Dispatch* that generated two National Baseball Hall of Fame writers—J. Roy Stockton and Bob Broeg—produced another one recently in Rick Hummel. Broeg hired Hummel—a University of Missouri grad—after his discharge from the army and assigned him to the Cardinals beat. There, Hummel learned his craft, which is much more than just watching a ball game and retelling the story.

Hummel, nicknamed the Commish for his leadership in sports statistical leagues he has been involved with over the years, is meticulous in his stories, which he still writes as a senior sports columnist for the *Post-Dispatch*. Through the years he's covered more than four thousand games, and over that time consistently displayed objectivity. "That very first day covering the Cardinals I realized I could no longer be a fan. I like certain players and I'm glad for them when they do well, but I don't root for any team," said Hummel. "I mean, I'm happy when the Cardinals win, but I'm not unhappy when they lose."

Hummel has the total respect of the men he covers daily. Count among them fellow Cardinal Hall of Famer Whitey "The White Rat" Herzog. He commended Hummel on his ability to keep an open mind until he found the truth. "Commish was always fair. He'd print the truth,

and I never had a problem with that. Hell, the truth is the truth. He's intelligent about the game and always asked well-thought-out questions."

A future Hall of Fame manager concurred. For "Professor" Tony LaRussa, a reporter needs to be on his toes intellectually or he'll look foolish. No need to wonder with Hummel. "Rick is very honest and he will tell you what's wrong," stated LaRussa. "He does what he has to do, he respects the game and the people in and around the game."

Hummel has covered virtually every sport. As of this writing, those include thirty-one World Series, twenty-nine baseball All-Star Games, a pair of NCAA basketball Final Fours, and at least one world championship boxing match. He expanded into other forms of media as well, co-hosting a show on KFNS Radio in St. Louis with fellow baseball reporter John Marecek called "The First Pitch," a later show called "The Baseball Bunch" with Cardinals television broadcaster Jay Randolph, and numerous guest spots on KMOX, KFNS, and Fox Sports Midwest, TV home of the Cardinals.

The press box at Busch Stadium was named the Bob Broeg–Rick Hummel Press Box, complete with a plaque and picture on the door as you enter. Rick Hummel was inducted into the writers' wing of the National Baseball Hall of Fame in 2007, receiving the J.G. Taylor Spink Award.

Left, top: Rick Hummel poses with Rev. Jackie Brock and Lou Brock at the J. G. Taylor Spink Award exhibit at Cooperstown after Hummel's dedication.

Left, bottom: Hummel shows off the Bob Broeg–Rick Hummel Press Box.

TIM McCARVER

Ford C. Frick Award Winner 2012

The St. Louis Cardinals recognized early that Tim McCarver had the qualities of enthusiasm and leadership to become a top-tier major league catcher. Signed to a then large bonus in 1959 by the Cardinals, he spent three seasons shuttling between St. Louis and a trio of farm clubs, but was clearly being groomed as the catcher of the future. In '63 he stuck and began a run that included three trips to the World Series and two world championships.

McCarver was an excellent broadcaster, first at WPHL-TV in Philadelphia, and then as a backup NBC Game of the Week color commentator in 1980. What attracted the national TV executives was the depth of Tim's analysis of the action, more so than any other color man up to that time.

But what groomed his exceptional talent at the microphone were those playing days, twenty-one seasons worth, in St. Louis, Philadelphia (nine years), Montreal, back to St. Louis (two seasons), Boston, and back to Philadelphia, ending in 1980. His commanding style behind the plate gave his pitchers confidence in calling the game.

Two Hall of Famers in particular demanded that McCarver be their receiver every time out—Cardinals pitcher Bob Gibson and Cardinals/Phillies pitcher Steve Carlton. The temperamental

Gibson expected twenty-four-year-old Timmy Mac to follow instructions, not try to lead the way. Gibby posted 18 or more wins in eight of the next ten seasons with McCarver.

However, McCarver's great strength with the Cardinals was his bat, and his ability in the clutch. In the '64 World Series he hit a sizzling .478 with five runs batted in and finished second in the MVP voting to his buddy Gibson. In the '67 season, he was central to the Cardinals offense, hitting .295 with 14 homers and 65 runs batted in with a slugging percentage of .452. He finished second in the National League MVP voting to teammate Orlando Cepeda.

Back in the '64 World Series, one can't forget his game-winning, tenth-inning three-run homer at Yankee Stadium in Game 5 after the Cardinals had given up a 2–0 lead with Gibson pitching in the ninth inning. *Post-Dispatch* writer Bob Broeg said, "That home run won the Series for the Cardinals for sure."

A little trivia: not many catchers in baseball history have led their league in triples but McCarver did in 1966. He banged out nine triples to lead the NL.

McCarver had plenty of baseball left in him when he was traded to Philadelphia. In total

FORD C. FRICK AWARD
2012
Tim McCarver

Tim McCarver made a seamless transition from the playing field to the broadcast booth after a successful 21-year career in the big leagues, thanks to his knowledge of the game and his natural passion for analyzing the sport. His down-home style and fan-friendly analysis has kept him in the national spotlight for more than four decades with four national networks, earning him national praise and recognition for his broadcasting prowess.

Born in Memphis, Tenn., McCarver was a gifted high school athlete who made his big league debut with the St. Louis Cardinals in 1959 – the same year he signed with the club out of high school. He was the starting catcher for a Redbirds club that won three National League pennants and two World Series in the 1960s, and also played for the Phillies, Expos and Red Sox.

With his playing career complete, the articulate McCarver quickly joined the Phillies broadcast team as an analyst. After moving to the Mets in 1983 for a regular broadcasting assignment, McCarver attracted the attention of the national networks and began working for NBC and then ABC. When CBS took over Major League Baseball's national package in 1990, McCarver was selected as its lead analyst, finding an audience appreciative of his ability to simplify the game.

After four years with CBS, McCarver worked with The Baseball Network in 1994-95 before heading to FOX in 1996, as the emerging network would become baseball's new home for marquee events. During this time, McCarver maintained his position with the Mets through 1998, moving to the Yankees' broadcast team from 1999-2001 and then to the Giants in 2002. His 22 World Series assignments are the most for an analyst in the television era.

His sharp wit, catchy one-liners and insistence on keeping the game fun made McCarver a fixture on baseball's national TV presence for multiple generations of fans.

National Baseball Hall of Fame and Museum, Inc.

Cooperstown, New York
July 21, 2012

he played in six postseasons; however, the Phillies never got past the National League Championship Series, losing three straight times. He holds a unique distinction of having been one of just twenty-nine players to play in the major leagues in four different decades—the 1950s to 1980s.

McCarver's broadcast career was planned, offered by the Phillies as early as 1977, to be effective upon retirement which came in 1980. He credits his mentors at Philadelphia for his education and training in the field. The legendary Harry Kalas, Andy Musser, Chris Wheeler, and colorful star center fielder Richie Ashburn molded his booth delivery.

By 1983 another step came when the top market in the country wanted Mac's services as the analyst of the New York Mets television network. By now, McCarver had a reputation as "the ballplayer in the booth" who could give an on-field perspective of what just happened and why or what should happen next. He's given credit for having set new standards of baseball savvy needed to be a great analyst. An example that's given happened in 1989 when the Cardinals played the Mets and their new pitching ace Frank Viola. New York had a 4-2 lead in the bottom of the ninth.

When the Cardinals' Tom Pagnozzi hit a fly ball that moved base runner Milt Thompson from second to third, the audience thought "no big deal." But Mets announcer McCarver pointed out what a big deal that little play could be.

"If the next hitter, Vince Coleman, gets on first, now he can steal second as the tying run, which doesn't happen without Thompson's alert tag up."

So what followed? Coleman singled to cut the lead to 4–3, but Ozzie Smith made the third out as Coleman was stealing second. The point was made: McCarver had properly set the table for the viewers, giving them a more entertaining perspective of the game's strategy.

His term with the Mets lasted from 1983 to 1998, while he built his Hall of Fame reputation on national games. Here's the list of his national assignments: NLCS reporter on ABC (1984), Monday Night Baseball backup team (1984–1989), with Jack Buck on CBS (1990–1991), with Sean McDonough (1992–1993), and then with his great friend Joe Buck (1996–2013). Then there were all those World Series.

He's also covered freestyle skiing at the 1988 Olympics and co-hosted prime-time coverage on CBS, as well as in 1992. Amazingly, he's the only broadcaster in history to broadcast on a regular basis the Mets, Yankees, and Phillies—three great rivals.

Long ago he passed the late Curt Gowdy, a legendary broadcaster who worked 13 World Series. In all, McCarver broadcast 23 World Series. Ironically, his first was as a last-minute replacement for Howard Cosell on the 1985 Cardinals–Kansas City Royals pairing, and his career ended with his beloved Cardinals in 2013 against the Boston Red Sox.

Fox Network's number one star and St. Louisan, Joe Buck, partnered with McCarver for sixteen World Series and eighteen seasons total.

"It's been nothing but a treat, and I owe him more than I can express for being the best audience, the best partner," summarized Joe Buck. "He'd run through a wall for whoever is on his team. That was the case when he was playing and that's the case when he's broadcasting."

Tim McCarver, who broadcast baseball for thirty seasons, was awarded the Ford C. Frick Award for excellence in baseball broadcasting by the Baseball Hall of Fame in 2012.

J. Roy Stockton was not a model student. He quit college to cover a boxing match back in 1915 and went on to follow the St. Louis Federal League baseball team in Cuba. But J. Roy Stockton could spin a story and became nationally known for his witty style in a series of profiles in the *Saturday Evening Post*, which was compiled into a book in 1945 titled *The Gashouse Gang and a Couple of Other Guys*. Two other books he had a hand in writing were *My Kind of Baseball*, by Rogers Hornsby, and *Frank Frisch: The Fordham Flash*.

Born in 1896, the McKinley High School (St. Louis) graduate came on board the *St. Louis Post-Dispatch* in 1917 and would remain for forty years as a sportswriter and later sports editor. Today, print journalists commonly moonlight as broadcasters, but it was unusual before 1950. Stockton took part in what may have been the first remote broadcast of a sporting event when he was one of the commentators on a radio broadcast of the 1947 United States Amateur Golf Championship held at St. Louis Country Club. He would later spend fifteen years hosting an evening radio show on local affiliate KSD Radio.

In 1926 he jumped on the Cardinals' bandwagon after covering golf and other sports. When Rogers Hornsby led the Cardinals to their first world championship in 1926, Stockton was hooked on the Redbirds. His prolific career got another boost when, in 1932, he was elected president of the Baseball Writers' Association of America, the organization commissioned to elect players to Cooperstown.

His level of respect peaked in 1951, when baseball was looking for a new commissioner. Suddenly, one of America's best-known and most respected sportswriters, Red Smith, nominated Stockton to be the next commissioner of baseball. This was no willy-nilly publicity stunt; Smith meant it. "Stockton is a man of many gifts and integrity," Smith began. "His years as one of the country's finest baseball writers has given him a rich background of experience and knowledge." The job went to Ford C. Frick, who became the namesake of an award given to broadcasters elected to the Hall of Fame.

Stockton was a giant in the sports reporting industry. He set the example for excellence and had the help of a great baseball franchise that frequently put his words in the national spotlight. In the end, he did what many dream of, moving to the warm weather in Florida where he lived the rest of his life—some fourteen years—until leukemia ended his life in 1972 at age seventy-nine.

J. Roy Stockton is remembered in St. Louis by the St. Louis Chapter of the Baseball Writers' Association of America every January. There is a specific award given for outstanding achievement in baseball called the J. Roy Stockton Award. He set the table for the next two great St. Louis Hall of Fame sportswriters, Bob Broeg and Rick Hummel. In 1972 Stockton was selected for the J. G. Taylor Spink Award, placing him into the writers' wing of the Hall of Fame in Cooperstown.

BIBLIOGRAPHY

Thanks to the living Hall of Famers, some of whom graciously shared their stories for this book. And thanks to the collectors, who contributed items of memorabilia to add to the book's historical perspective.

Books

Broeg, Bob. *The Pilot Light and the Gas House Gang*. St. Louis: The Bethany Press, 1980.

Broeg, Bob, and Jerry Vickery. *St. Louis Cardinals Encyclopedia*. Chicago: Masters Press, 1998.

Craft, David, and Tom Owens. *Redbirds Revisited—Great Memories and Stories from St. Louis Cardinals*. Chicago: Bonus Books, Inc., 1990.

Freese, Mel. *The Glory Years of the St. Louis Cardinals*. St. Louis: Palmerston & Reed Publishing Company, 1999.

Gibson, Bob, with Lonnie Wheeler. *Stranger to the Game: The Autobiography of Bob Gibson*. New York: Penguin, 1994.

Hanks, Stephen. *150 Years of Baseball*. Publications International, Ltd., 1989.

Heidenry, John. *The Gashouse Gang*. New York: Public Affairs, 2008.

Honig, Donald. *The St. Louis Cardinals: An Illustrated History*. New York: Prentice Hall, 1991.

Hood, Robert E. *The Gashouse Gang: The Incredible Madcap St. Louis Cardinals of 1934*. New York: William Morrow Company, Inc., 1976.

Horrigan, Kevin. *White Rat: A Life in Baseball*. New York: Harper and Row, 1987.

Thomas, Joan M. *Baseball's First Lady: Helene Hathaway Robison Britton and the St. Louis Cardinals*. St. Louis: Reedy Press, 2010.

Thomas, Joan M. *St. Louis' Big League Ballparks*. Arcadia Publishing, 2004.

Internet Sources

TheBaseballPage.com, bigwalnuthistory.org, baseball-reference.com, baseballguru.com, Baseball-Almanac.com, brainyquote.com, baseballLibrary.com, nyfuturestars.com, RogersHornsby.com, The Baseball Biography Project, hickoksports.com, thebaseballcube.com, johnnymize.com, answers.com, entertainment.howstuffworks.com, cmgww.com, pabook.libraries.psu.edu, sportsecyclopedia.com, spiritus-temporis.com, journalism.missouri.edu, sportswriters.net, baseball-fever.com, negroleaguebaseball.com, forbes.com, herald-review.com

PHOTO CREDITS

St. Louis Cardinals media guides, scorecards, and yearbooks: front cover, ii (foreground), iii, iv, vi, 45 (bottom), 52 (bottom left), 53 (left), 68 (bottom), 91, 95, 104, 110 (right), 118, 134, 135 (bottom), 176, 184, 194–195, 198, 199, 200, 201, 203, 204, 205, 207, 216

Author collection: ii (background), v, 2–3, 4, 5, 6, 7, 14 (bottom), 30, 34 (top), 35 (top), 44 (right), 52 (top and bottom right), 53 (right), 66, 68 (top left), 69, 76, 77 (inset), 84 (right), 85 (inset), 88, 89, 90 (left), 92, 94, 106 (top), 110 (left), 111 (right), 116, 119 (top), 158, 160, 169, 180, 196, 206, 208 (top)

Library of Congress: 10, 20, 56, 70, 102, 114, 124, 144, 148, 149, 150–151, 154, 156, 157, 162, 164, 165, 170, 172, 174, 177, 178

National Baseball Hall of Fame and Museum: front cover, 8–9, 11, 12, 13, 14 (bottom), 15, 16, 17, 18, 19, 21, 22, 23, 24, 25, 26, 27, 29, 32, 33, 34 (bottom), 35 (bottom, left and right), 36, 37, 38, 39, 40, 42, 43, 45, 46, 47, 48, 49, 50, 51, 54, 55, 57, 59, 59, 60–61, 62, 63, 64, 65, 67, 68, 71, 72, 73, 74, 75, 77 (background), 78, 79, 80, 81, 83, 87, 93, 96–97, 98, 99, 100, 101, 103, 105, 108, 109, 112, 113, 115, 117, 120, 121, 122, 123, 125, 126, 127, 128, 129, 130, 131, 132, 133, 136, 137, 138, 139, 141, 142, 143, 145, 146, 147, 152, 153, 155, 159, 163, 166, 167, 171, 173, 175, 176, 179, 181, 182, 183, 185, 186, 187, 189, 190, 192, 210, 211, 212, 213

St. Louis Globe-Democrat, by the Mercantile Library at the University of Missouri–St. Louis: 41, 106 (bottom), 107 (background), 111 (left), 119 (bottom), 161, 202, 214

John George Medwick: 31, 82, 84 (left), 85 (background)

Topps: front cover, 44 (left), 90 (right), 95 (top), 107 (inset), 135 (top), 168

UPI Photo/Bill Greenblatt: 208 (bottom), 209

Bob Briggs, by Linda Briggs-Harty: 86

Missouri History Museum: 188

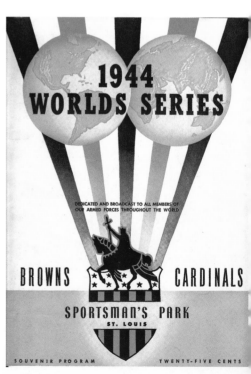

ABOUT THE AUTHORS

Greg Marecek, sports historian and media figure, has four St. Louis sports books to his credit. In addition to *The Cardinals of Cooperstown*, Greg has done two books on the St. Louis Hawks and one on the St. Louis Football Cardinals. He is also president of the St. Louis Sports Hall of Fame.

Myron Holtzman, the last sports editor of the *St. Louis Globe-Democrat*, also has worked for the *Sporting News*, the Associated Press, and Anheuser-Busch where he was publications manager for the St. Louis Cardinals. He is currently PR director for the St. Louis Sports Hall of Fame.